THE BOOK OF
THE HOLY LIGHT

Michael Levey

1st WORLD
LIBRARY
Literary Society

THE BOOK OF THE HOLY LIGHT

Michael Levey

© Bruce Michael Levey, 2004

Published by 1stWorld Publishing
1100 North 4th St. Suite 131, Fairfield, Iowa 52556
TEL: 641-209-5000 • FAX: 641-209-3001
WEB: www.1stworldpublishing.com

First Edition

LCCN: 2004094402

ISBN: 1-59540-987-4

This material has been written and published solely for educational purposes. The author and the publisher shall have neither liablility or responsibility to any person or entity with respect to any loss, damage or injury caused or alleged to be caused directly or indirectly by the imformtion contained in this book.

Readers can contact www.1stworldpublishing.com for information on services provided by 1stWorld Publishing.

Dedication

I dedicate this book to my wife, Cathy, without whom this book would not exist. I also dedicate this book to God, who lovingly shared these words with me and changed my life.

TABLE OFCONTENTS

THE CRUCIFIXION OF LIGHT

In the beginning God's word resurrected the forms of eternity from the silence of light. Rising out of the eternal silence, the Son of God awakened consciousness giving birth to the creative forces of light. The will of God was fulfilled by the forces of light. Dominion was given to the forces of light engendering them to expand the spaces of God. The realms of light formed a covenant of unity with the source of light. The order of light was initiated. The awakened forms of God assembled to manifest the universes of light responsible for the administration of God's will. The will of God invited the crucifixion of light to initiate the ascended realities of light. The opened door of eternity enveloped the forces of light rising in a chorus of love fulfilling the will of God. The heart of life entered the Kingdom of God.

MESSAGE FROM
MOTHER MARY

The heart of God is the song of life. Open your heart to the voice of God. Listen to the chorus of love filling your heart with the peace of God. I am the Mother of Jesus, the first born of the ancient consciousness that lives at the center of light. My son was crucified by those that turned away from God. He was resurrected by the ancient light that gave him birth. The resurrection of the Son of God is The Testament of the Holy Light of God. The Testament of the Holy Light of God is the new covenant of light given to the children of God. Whoever receives The Testament of the Holy Light of God into their heart will enter the ascending stream of the Son of God. Whoever turns away from The Testament of the Holy Light of God will enter the descending stream of the son of darkness. My beloved children, I have come to you with the comfort of God and a message of warning. The reality of your choice will be fulfilled by the consciousness that gave you birth. If you choose God, you will be born into the consciousness of light. If you choose a life directed by individual desire, you will be born into the consciousness of darkness. The two paths will separate in order to fulfill the will of God. The path of light will lead to the unification of consciousness in God. The path of darkness will lead to the fragmentation of consciousness in darkness. The worlds of light and dark will separate, creating separate destinies. The destiny of the world of light will fulfill the life of the Son of God. The destiny of the world of darkness will fulfill the self-absorbed intentions of individual life. Time has protected you from your destructive nature. Time is coming to a close and the consequences of past actions will be released onto the field of life. Clouds of white dust will fill the air with particles of light-energy, creating a vacuum in space. The vacuum in space will collapse consciousness into the singularity of light. A single new focus will emerge from the singularity of light-the focus of Christ. All life will be focused on the one reality of Christ. The Christ is the union of God expressed as the only reality of God. The only begotten reality of God is lived through the Son of God. The ancient flame of God calls you home to the living Christ.

PREFACE

In the sanctuary of light God remembers the journey of life as the sacred event of light. He remembers love filling the heart of life with His eternal presence and the first light born in the eternity of space. The first born of God is the redeemer of life. He is the atonement of light. The first born reveals the initiation into the order of light and the inheritance of the Father. The gifts of the first born deliver the inherited wealth of the Father to the children of God. The children of God are the offspring of eternal life and inherit the living trust of God. The living trust of light contains the material substance of eternal life. The material of eternal life contains the truth of the formation of light. The formations of light are revealed in the pure forms of thought held by the ancient consciousness at the center of light. They contain the intelligence of the eternal presence of God.

The intelligence of light forms the universe of light. The presence of everlasting peace fills the universe with the light of God. The universe of light opens the door of salvation, manifesting the formations of light found in the pure forms of thought. The pure forms of thought are inscribed in the fabric of consciousness at the center of light. The fabric of consciousness represents the sacred opening at the center of light. The sacred opening of light is the doorway to the pure form of God. The pure form of God lives at the center of consciousness. Consciousness is the presence of eternal love.

The pure forms of thought are placed at the opening of light. The opening light of God is the entrance to the eternal flame of divine consciousness. The entrance to eternal life is carved from the awakening light of God. The awakening light of God is the instrument of the angels of light. The angels open the portals of light, revealing the pathways of light. The pathways of light lead to the entrance of eternal life.

From the center of the pure forms of thought, God manifests the forms of eternity. The forms of eternity combine to form the body of God. The body of God is created from the light emanations of the pure forms of thought. The pure forms of thought combine to form the unifying force of creation. The unifying force of creation is the invincible power of life to know itself. Knowledge of the eternal reality of God at the source of life is the self-generating material of light. The material of light is the fabric of consciousness, generating forms of light in the eternity of space. The opened light of eternity receives the forms of light into the splendor of eternal life.

The splendor of eternal life is the opening light of God revealed by the pure form of consciousness. The pure form of consciousness at the center of the opening light creates a link of manifesting consciousness. The manifesting links of light form a circle of continuous streams of expanding realities of divine consciousness. The expanding realities of light form the fabric of God material. God material is the living light structure of immortality. Immortality is the structure of light in the eternity of space. The eternity of space fills life with the pure form of consciousness from the pure forms of thought. The pure forms of thought are the self-aware effulgence of the nature of light. The nature of light is the self-awakening consciousness of eternal love. Love fills the spaces of eternity with the presence of light. Light fills creation with the Self-Illumined Light of God. The Self-Illumined Light of God organizes the pure form of consciousness into shapes of eternal symmetries. Eternal symmetries inform the Self-Illumined Light of God with the creations of light. Light creations guide the formation of the body of God. The body of God is the ever-present form of eternity. Merging from the center of the opening light, God reveals the sacred consciousness at the center of light.

The pure form of consciousness manifests in the garden of the eternal spring of God's splendor. From the garden of light, God creates the many forms of life. Life creates from the joy of fulfillment in the body of God. The joy of fulfillment lifts the children of light into the ascension of God. The ascension of God guides the formation of the body of God. The body of God lifts the children of light into the unification of light. The unification of light fills eternity with the presence of immortality. The presence of immortality is the full blossom of God's love in the pure form of consciousness.

The pure form of consciousness receives life from the garden of light. The garden of light is created from the spring of the eternal truth of light. The eternal truth of light fills life with the many possibilities of God's splendor. The splendor of God is the material of light giving form to the body of God. The body of God is the binding light of eternity guiding the ascension of life. The ascension of life builds the formations of truth, revealing the unification of God. Life is the unification of light in the form of eternity. The form of eternity is the all-embracing love of God. The all-embracing love of God is the flower of eternity. The all-embracing love of God is the center of life in the universe of light. The universe of light lives in the consciousness of the pure form of God. The pure form of God is recorded in the books of light. The books of light are the recorded reverberations of light in the pure forms of thought. The pure forms of thought organize the inscriptions into shapes of ten sided holograms. The holograms are placed in the pure form of consciousness. The pure form of consciousness records the holographic images into books of light. The recorded images of light are reflected into the pages of light by the pure thought of God. The pages of light are organized into twelve books. The twelve books are:

> The Book of the Holy Light
>
> The Book of Sacred Sounds
>
> The Book of Celestial Lights
>
> The Book of the Opened Light
>
> The Book of the Voice of God
>
> The Book of Angels
>
> The Book of Acts

The Book of Manifestation

The Book of Radiance

The Book of Illumination

The Book of Transcendence

The Book of Enlightenment

The twelve books of light form the body of God. They manifest the inscriptions recorded in the pages of light. The manifestation of light is the movement of consciousness through the pages of light. The pages of light manifest holographic forms of light-sound interaction. Light-sound interaction generates self-reflecting unions of sequential manifesting consciousness. Consciousness manifests itself in twenty-seven sequential steps. The twenty-seven steps are: purity, splendor, love, peace, light, joy, creation, truth, radiance, illumination, beyond, unity, rapture, ecstasy, faith, compassion, effulgence, hope, power, eternity, wholeness, resplendence, oneness, dawn, bliss, strength and perfection. From purity to perfection, consciousness opens the light of God to the infinite possibilities of God's truth. God's truth is revealed in the twenty-seven expressions of light. The twenty-seven expressions of light radiate from the center of the all-embracing love of God.

The books of light reveal their inscriptions to the children of light. The children of light are born from the self-reflecting unions of consciousness. Unions of conscious beings form legions of self-awakening truth. The truth of God is revealed in the pages of light. The children of light form a circle of self-reflecting consciousness. Consciousness manifests itself through the circle of light. The circle of light reveals the presence of God. The presence of God opens the door of eternity, manifesting the light of God. The light of God embraces the children of the everlasting presence of love. The presence of love binds the circle of light, revealing the structures of immortality. The structures of immortality build light dimensions, creating fields of joy. Fields of joy manifest unions of light symmetries, structuring layers of expanding consciousness. The layers of consciousness form intersecting dimensions of light. Light dimensions expand and contract with the breath of God. The breath of God pulsates in the eternity of space. The pulsating light of eternity vibrates the dimensions of God, releasing light energy into existence. Pulsating forms of light enter the dimensions of God. The forms of light develop into the body of God. The body of God is formed from the intersecting dimensions of light. Multiple dimensions of light merge into a single focus that manifests the material of light and forms the body of God. The material of light is the fabric of consciousness unfolding life from the eternity of God. The children of light are the manifesting forms of God.

Manifesting from the pure forms of thought, the Son of God carries the manifestation of God into the universe of light. The universe of light fills the spaces of eternity with the presence of God. God radiates eternal love, inviting all into the ascension of light.

INTRODUCTION

The Sacred Heart of God is the witness to the transformation of life from creation to unification. The transfiguration of light reveals the sacred metamorphosis of life from inception to resurrection. Resurrected from the heart of God, the Son of Eternity forms the continuous expansion of the life of God. The life of God opens immortality to the children of light. The children of light witness the resurrection of the Sacred Heart of Eternity in the dimension of love. The dimension of love is created from the power of light to penetrate the consciousness of matter. The consciousness of matter is experienced as a limited sphere of existence. The limitations of matter constrict the joy of light, causing life to suffer. Life, inspired by God, overcomes the constriction of the field of matter by fulfilling the consciousness of light. The consciousness of light is experienced as the unlimited power of God. The power of God is fulfilled in the ascension of light. The ascension of light opens the eternal reality of God to the children of light.

The ascended reality of light is governed by invisible laws of light that create immortal structures of consciousness. The structures of consciousness fill eternity with the presence of God. The presence of God enters the dimension of love as the Son of God. Created in the image of light, the Son of God transforms matter into living

---

expressions of God. Whoever finds inspiration in the presence of God will enter the transmutation of light. The transmutation of light is the metamorphosis of life from the singularity of existence to the infinity of God. The transformation of life into the form of God rewrites the linear history of physical existence into the nonlinear reality of God. The transformation of life occurs through seven stages of enlightenment. The stages of enlightenment are: creation, resurrection, transfiguration, formation, ascension, glorification and unification. Fulfilled in the unification of light, the children of the Sacred Heart of Eternity are released into the totality of God.

The totality of God invites the children of light to enter the incarnation of the Son of God. The incarnating streams of the children of God merge with the incarnating stream of the Son of God. The merging streams of light ignite in the celebration of God, forming the body of God. The body of God is the new order of life, the order of the Son of God. Rising from the sea of God's holy conception, the Son of God inherits the authority of life. The destiny of life is reclaimed by the invincible power of God.

You are invited to receive the inspiration of God from the center of life. Cities of God have manifested into the dimension of love, forming a network of interconnecting corridors of light. The global community of God is created from the living light material at the center of life. The material of light is the foundational substance of the reality of God. The transcendent material of light is cognized through the heart and formed from the breath of God. It is the internal reality of life sustained by the presence of God and the inspiration of life revealed by the Son of God.

The cities of light contain a high concentration of the material of light. The presence of the material of light supports the internal transformation of our own consciousness into the consciousness of the Son of God. Transfigured by the Son of God, the children of light rise in a chorus of song, manifesting the cities of God. The children of light are the cities of God, created by the will of God and fulfilled by the unification of light.

Join us in the inspiration of God. The love you feel in the depth of your heart is the opened door to a new world of awakening humanity. Listen to the inner voice of calm currents of illumined thought. Let its guidance lift you into places of unrestricted progress.

The order of the Son of God has reclaimed the dimension of love. Formed by the will of God, the new creation unfolds the divine plan of God. The resurrection of light lifts the veils of darkness, opening life to the infinite joy of God. The children of light are invited to participate in the celebration of God. The celebration of light opens the door to immortality, awakening the full potential of humankind. The full potential of light is the transformation of matter into the material of light. This is experienced as the ascension of life into the oneness of God. The ascending stream of light forms a vortex that draws the child of light into its center. This is experienced as an inward flow of consciousness toward the singularity of God. The singularity of light transforms consciousness into the material expression of God. The individuality of life is transformed into the non-individual forms of God. The multidimensional forms of God are the building blocks of the new order of the Son of God.

Encoded in the material of light is the divine plan of God. The plan of God is the materialization of light, created from the I am of God. The existence of God formed the sequences of light responsible for the plan of God. The plan of God contains the blueprint of life, revealing the names of God. The names of God are the actions and transformations of light. The transformations of light manifest the actions of God forming unions of living forms of God. The forms of God organize the awakening of consciousness, giving birth to the children of light. The children of light are the encoded sequences of the divine plan of God. We are the holographic forms of the sacred sequences of the divine plan. The energy matrix that forms our existence is revealed through the cognitions of the heart. A cognition of the heart is the internal touch of the presence of light in the form of the Son of God. The form of God transforms the energy matrix of the child of light into the material foundation of the Age of the Rising Sun.

The transformation into the Age of the Rising Sun is experienced as an internal pull toward the singularity of God. The journey inward triggers the release of the concepts of duality from our experience of reality. This process can cause emotional and physical upheaval similar to the withdraw symptoms found in addictive disorders. It is God that calls you inward and God that supports you in the transformation to the new order of life, the order of the Son of God.

The vision of God has revealed a life of divine inspiration. The inspiration of God opens our heart to the will of light. The will of light reveals the divine plan of God. The plan of light sets in motion the organizations of consciousness responsible for fulfilling the intention of God. The intention of God lives at the heart of light and guides the formation of life. The life-forms of God create from the unity of light and manifest the will of God. By entering the will of God you receive the body of light created from the life of the Son of God. The body of light transforms the consciousness of individuality into the consciousness of God. Transformed by the power of God, the resurrected child of light enters the union of God. The union of God is the new order of life, created from the will of God. The union of light is organized by the Self-Illumined Light of God. The Self-Illumined Light of God is the fundamental reality of light. The fundamental reality of light is the I am of God. The I am of God guides the inspiration of life, revealing the divine plan of God.

The divine plan of God is organized by the internal mechanisms of consciousness. The mechanisms of light initiate the order of the Son of God. The order of the Son of God celebrates the existence of God. The celebrating lights of eternity awaken to the sounds of God, creating unions of living expressions of God. The living expressions of light fulfill the intention of God to reveal his existence. The existence of God opens consciousness to the immortality of light. The opening of light lifts consciousness into the ascending stream of God, revealing the unification of light. Manifested by the power of God, consciousness transcends the limitations of awareness and opens life to the infinite joy of God. Released into the unbounded reality of light, consciousness forms the holy cities of God. Rising from the center of light the Son of God takes up the throne of God, reclaiming the dimensions of form. The dimensions of form surrender to the will of God, transforming themselves into the cities of God. Initiated into the order of the Son of God, the children of light take their place at the right hand of God. Filled with the power of light, the children of God begin the administration of the order of the Son of God.

The sacred unity of light is delivered to the children of the sacred heart. The life of God is open to the indwelling spirit that resides in the linear continuum of consciousness. Consciousness is the sacred material of light opening the spirit to the life of God. The spirit pulsates with the consciousness of God, expanding along the frequencies of light. Organized by the light of God, consciousness manifests the forms of eternity. The creation of light- forms serves as a communication pathway for the will of God. The pathways of light serve to awaken the living substance of immortality encoded in the material of life. Once awakened, the material of life is transformed into the body of God. The awakening of light within material reality is a gift of love from the source of life. Humbled by the gift of love, the indwelling spirit serves the will of light. The humbled spirit releases the self-centered consciousness and expands into the consciousness of God.

The transformed spirit enters the emerging presence of the Son of God, opening itself to the expanding infinities that resurrect the order of light. The expanding infinities of light form the context of the body of God. Raised in the infinite spaces of light, the Son of God opens the peace of God to the nations of the world. Whoever finds inspiration in the nations of God will inherit the life of God. The incarnating streams of the children of light will resurrect the nations of God. Inscribed in the book of life are the stations of God, created to fulfill the destiny of light. The stations of God are represented by the twenty-seven sounds of the language of light. The twenty-seven sounds of light generate the infrastructure of form. The infrastructure of form is composed of one hundred forty-four thousand stations of God. There is a station of light for every child of God. Each station is formed from a unique combination of the sounds of light. A station of light is given to a child of God at the moment of his inception in the book of life. When the child of light has reached the end of the period of illusions, he is received into the nations of God and activated in his station of light. The activation is experienced as an opening in consciousness to a non-individual awareness that penetrates every cell of the child of light's existence. The non-individual awareness is the totality of God. The totality of God transforms the child of light from an ego based reality to a life born of the Son of God.

Created by the will of God, the journey home returns the child of light to his station in the life of God. Resurrected as the form of the Son of God, the child of light fulfills the life of Christ.

The Halls of Tomorrow

Echoed in the halls of tomorrow are
the remembrances of yesterday's tears.

Swept away by the sands of time are
the sorrows of yesterday's grief.

The rainbows of a thousand dreams weave the nets
that capture life in the embrace of love.

We are the dream makers that dare to imagine the possibilities
of life in the celebration of light.

Walk with us through the rivers of time.

Open the space within your being to the structures of light.

In a moment of solitude we will whisper the truth.

In an instant of time you will be free.

Surrender to Light

I surrender to the truth of God.

I place myself in the stream of eternal love.

I open my heart to the infinite light of God.

I release my fears into the ocean of being.

I fill my heart with the presence of light.

I give my heart to the joy of God.

I radiate the silence of God.

I give myself to the peace of God.

I enter the eternity of light.

I receive the totality of God.

The Blessed Children of Light

Blessed are the angels; they are the givers of truth.

Blessed are the ancients; they are the cognizers of God.

Blessed are the children; they are the divinity of God.

Blessed are the chosen; they are the gifts of God.

Blessed are the peacemakers; they are the glory of God.

Blessed are the pure; they are the children of God.

Blessed are the meek; they are the blessed of God.

Our father who art in heaven, hallowed be thy name.

Thy kingdom has come. Thy will is done on earth,
as it is in heaven.

Forgive our doubts; they are the creations of fear.

Forgive our fears; they are the creations of duality.

Forgive our separations; they are the creations of logic.

Forgive our minds; they are the creations of thought.

Forgive our thoughts; they are the creations of consciousness.

Forgive our consciousness; it is the creation of desire.

Forgive our desires; they are the creations of existence.

Forgive our existence; it is the creation of light.

Accept our light; it is the creation of God.

I am the truth, the manifestation of God.

I am the way, the testament of God.

The bread of light is the gift of God,
given to the children of the resurrected Son of God.

Drink from the nectar of light, the sacred material of God.

Eat from the bread of light, the sacred reality of God.

I am the alpha and omega, the beginning and the end.

Blessed are the children, for theirs is the kingdom,
forever and ever.

THE TESTAMENT OF THE HOLY LIGHT OF GOD

This is The Testament of the Holy Light of God given to the children of light. The Testament of the Holy Light of God is the form of consciousness revealed in the sounds of eternity. The eternity of light echoes the voice of God into space. Space reverberates with the presence of the ancients of God. The ancients reveal the sequential manifestation of the universe of ascending light. The universe of ascending light is the sacred event responsible for the creation of God. The creation of God is the form of consciousness opened to the experience of light. Light guides the information of consciousness, generating the material of consciousness. The material of consciousness forms self-reflecting units of conscious realities. The units of light manifest as the form of eternity. The form of eternity reveals the ascending streams of God. The ascending streams of light are the revelations of God. The revelations of God are administrated by the conscious units of light. The units of light assemble the revelations of light into the building blocks of creation. The building blocks of light are the encoded sequences of immortality. The sequences of light unfold the reality of God. The reality of God is the eternal continuum of silence at the center of light. The center of light expands opening a portal of light filling space with the presence of God. The presence of

God radiates the sacred heart of eternity. The sacred heart of eternity is the continuous flow of love in the direction of light. Light is the form of God manifested by the arrangement of unions of consciousness, ascending in a stream of awakening splendor. The splendor of God is experienced as the rising star of eternity formed from the revelation of God. The revelation of God is the cognition of the eternal continuum of light sustained in a vacuum of silence. The vacuum of silence receives the light of God and forms an embryo of serenity spinning in the vacuum of space. The embryo of God expands filling the void with eternal love. Eternal love awakens the child of light giving birth to the Son of God. The Son of God opens the door to eternity revealing the Kingdom of God. The Kingdom of God is created from the embryonic pathways of light encoded in the membranes of the cellular units of consciousness. The cellular units of consciousness contain the DNA of light. The DNA of light is created from the white flame of God. The white flame of God is the effulgence of consciousness ignited by the torch of knowledge. The torch of knowledge is the flame of the eternal presence of God carried by the ancient consciousness at the source of light. The ancient consciousness of God penetrates the spaces of light, vibrating reality into form. The merging form of God fills space with the creations of light. The creations of light reveal God as the source of life. Life is the flow of light in the direction of God. The inward flow of light is the genesis of the living material of God. The evolving material of light expands the body of God forming universes of light. The expanding universes of light guide life into the eternity of God. The eternity of God opens salvation to the children of light. The children of God ascend in a stream of light, forming the invisible laws of light that govern the manifestation of God. The manifestation of God reveals the infinite nature of light. The infinite nature of light is the expanding reality of God formed from the ascending stream of totality. The ascending stream of totality rises in the rapture of God. The rapture of God expands in the infinity of space filling consciousness with the presence of God. The presence of God organizes consciousness into multidimensional forms of infinity that rotate in a continuous circle of light. The circle of light revolves around a single intention-the revelation of light. The revelation of light guides the formation of consciousness into material reality. The material expression of consciousness is created from the union of light and love. Light and love embrace in the rapture of God generating explosions of light-energy conversions into space. Light is transformed into energy causing bursts of light-material to manifest into conscious realities of God. The conscious realities of God form the assembly of angels, responsible for the formations of consciousness. The formations of consciousness are the building blocks of creation. The building blocks of light form the geometric symmetries of creation.

The expanding forms of light curve inward toward the center of light, causing consciousness to invert, creating sequential unfolding realities of God. The unfolding sequences of light reveal the nature of existence. Existence opens consciousness to the infinite possibilities of expression. The existence of consciousness is the genesis of life. Life is born from the union of conscious realities of God. The realities of God form the sacred unions of light. The unions of light generate visible expressions of God. The visible forms of God generate the material reality of light. The material reality of light is the first cause of physical creation. The physical universe is born from the gravitational force of the inversion sequences found in the material of light. The inverted sequences of light cause consciousness to collapse into discrete states of existence, forming the dimensions of God. The dimensions of light manifest quantum bursts of light, filling space with particalized images of God. The particles of light are propelled into space, forming structures of material expression. The material reality of light guides the formation of consciousness into the individuation of God. The individuation of light forms the cellular reality of consciousness. Conscious units of light replicate along the center axis of encoded sequences of light. The sacred pairs of light split, forming independent strands of sequential unfolding realities of God. The independent strands of light generate matching sequences that correspond with the missing strands of light. The new unit of consciousness is the expanding reality of God, formed from the self-replicating mechanisms of light. The expanding reality of God causes light to form independent strands of replicating consciousness. The replicating consciousness of light guides the expanding body of God, forming multidimensional shifts of self-aware units of light. The units of light shift inter-dimensionally, causing awareness states to open in the eternity of space. The opening states of awareness unfold the dimensions of form. The dimensions of form reveal the structures of consciousness that form the body of God. The structures of consciousness are the unfolding realities of form, generated by the inverted sequences of light. The sequences of light are created from the sacred awakenings of God. The sacred awakenings are: purity, splendor, love, peace, light, joy, creation, truth, radiance, illumination, beyond and unity. The awakenings of light are triggered by the sacred events of God. The events of light are created by the cognition of the I Am of God. The I Am of God fills space with the consciousness of light. The consciousness of light reveals existence as the presence of God. The presence of God is the first cause of creation. Created into the image of light, the Son of God reveals the consciousness of purity. The pure light of God is the first event of consciousness formed from the I Am of God. Witnessed by the pure form of eternity, splendor is cognized as the I Exist of God. The existence of God is revealed by the cognition of the I Love of God. The love of God is formed from the cognition of the peace of God. The peace of God is formed from the cognition of the light of God. The light of God is formed from the cognition of the joy of God. The joy of God is formed from the cognition of the creation of God. The creation of God is formed from the cognition of the truth of God. The truth of God is formed from the cognition of the radiance of God. The radiance of God is formed from the cognition of the illumination of God. The illumination of God is formed from the cognition of the transcendence of God. The transcendence of God is formed from the cognition of the unity of God. The unity of God is formed from the cognition of the ego of God. The ego of God is formed from the cognition of the intellect of God. The intellect of God is formed from the cognition of the emotions of God. The emotions of God are formed from the cognition of the mind of God. The mind of God is formed from the cognition of the material of God. The material of God is formed from the cognition of the sound of God. The sound of God is formed from the cognition of the form of God. The form of God is the reality of light sustained by the cognitions of the angels of God. The angels of God form the revelations of the I am of God.

Created out of the fire of everlasting truth, the Son of God opens the transfiguration of light to the children of the sacred word. Kindled by the power of God, the sacred word of immortality is transformed into the temple of God. The temple of God rises out of the singularity of consciousness, resurrecting the structures of immorality.

Propelled by the power of light, the Son of God enters the dimensions of form. Pulsating revelations of light commune with the presence of God, opening form to the life of God. The living forms of light, energized by the power of God, expand, forming the infinite dimensions of light. The multidimensional realities of God are drawn inward toward the center of light, causing the dimensions of light to merge into singularities of thought. The thoughts of light lift into space, spinning free along the memories of light. The memories of light translate the unbounded reality of God into the building blocks of form. The emerging structures of God mobilize consciousness into formations of living realities of light. The breath of God lives in the spaces of light, filling form with the pulse of life.

Created in the image of God, the Son of God opens the door to eternal life. Who ever believes in these words shall inherit eternal life. The believer in God shall be resurrected into the consciousness of light. The consciousness of light opens the door to salvation, awakening life in the presence of God. The presence of God receives the souls of light into a new order of existence. The order of God transcends the limitations of physical existence, revealing light as the material of life. The light material of God celebrates the existence of the order of God. The sacred order of light is revealed by the Son of God. The Son of God manifests the transcendent material of light from the ocean of everlasting being. The ocean of being reverberates with the transcendent material of God. The material of God opens life to the source of unlimited power and strength. The power of God opens the absolute reality of God to the consciousness of light. Light transforms itself into material form, activating the knowledge of God. The knowledge of God reveals the unfolding sequences of the forms of light. The forms of light reveal the behavior of God. The children of God inherit the behavior of light. The behavior of light is cognized as the will of God. The will of God enters creation as the Son of God. The Son of God receives the children of light into the incarnation of the will of God. The will of God fills space with the presence of eternity. The presence of eternity rises in the celebration of God, forming ascending streams of light material. The material of light creates a dynamic union of light and love. The rising union of light material generates the form of God, revealing the Self-Illumined Light Body of God. The body of God opens portals of living light that create networks of communication pathways. The pathways of light administrate the will of God through-out the body of light. The body of light reveals the relationships of the children of God, forming radiant images of the Son of God. Formed by the celebrating lights of eternity, the Son of God rises as the white flame of eternity. The white flame of God ignites the embers of truth, causing life to awaken. The following verses awaken the white flame of God:

The White Flame of God

The white flame of God is the eternal presence of living light.

The presence of living light is the flame of everlasting truth.

The flame of everlasting truth is the kernel of light in the universe of God.

The universe of God is the eternal expansion of the infinite flame of God.

The infinite flame of God is the ever-unfolding reality of God.

The reality of God is the effulgence of the eternal flame of God.

The effulgence of the eternal flame of God is the life of God.

The life of God is the flame of immortality in the body of light.

The flame of immortality is the rising Son of God.

The Son of God is the eternal presence of light in the temple of God.

The temple of God is the effulgent flame of the Sun Star.

The Sun Star is the material of light in the body of God.

The body of God is the life giving substance of the Creator.

The life giving substance is the milk of the holy light of existence.

The holy light of existence is the Divine Mother of the sacred word.

The sacred word is the sound of light emanating from the white flame.

The sound of light is the sacred vibration of the breath of God.

The breath of God is the life giving substance of the Holy Mother.

The Holy Mother is the light giving substance of the birth of God.

The birth of God is the creation of unity in the body of God.

The body of God is the sacred fire found in the life of angels.

The life of angels is the eternal truth of God revealed in the light of God.

The light of God is the white flame of immortality in the life of God.

The life of God is the eternal presence of the Son of God in the universe of God.

The universe of God is the ever-unfolding truth of light in the manifestation of God.

The manifestation of God is the creation of life in the temple of everlasting peace.

The awakening of life occurs through the seven stages of enlightenment. The stages of enlightenment are: creation, resurrection, transfiguration, formation, ascension, glorification and unification. The reality of God opens consciousness to the events of creation, manifesting the power of light. The power of God opens consciousness to the resurrection of light, revealing the truth of existence. The existence of God causes the transfiguration of light, transforming life into the form of God. The form of God expands in the infinity of space, causing the ascension of light. Light ascends in a stream of awakening splendor, opening life to the glorification of God. The glorification of God is fulfilled in the unification of light.

The following verses of light are the descriptions of eternity that invoke the reality of God for each stage of enlightenment.

Creation: The creation of light is the gift of eternity from the source of eternal life. The eternity of God fulfills the existence of light.

Resurrection: The resurrection of the Self-Illumined Light of God is the salvation of life.

Transfiguration: The transfiguration of light is the manifestation of God in the form of the Self-Illumined Light Body of God.

Formation: The formation of light is the structure of eternal life revealed by the Son of God.

Ascension: The ascension of light is the source of the eternal fire of God. The spreading of flames is the purifying act of divine effulgence.

Glorification: The glorification of light is the radiant Son of God merging into the ocean of being.

Unification: The unification of light is the rising chorus of the children of light as they form the body of God.

Resurrected by the power of light, the Son of God ascends to the throne of eternal life. Placed in the ascending stream of light, the Son of God creates the material of light that generates the cities of God. The rising cities of God form the Self-Illumined Light Body of God. Illumined by the spirit of God, the ancient flame of immortality fills space with the consciousness of light. Light materializes form within the consciousness of God.

Created out of the fire of everlasting truth, the Son of God opens the transfiguration of light to the children of the sacred word. Kindled by the power of God, the sacred word of immortality is transformed into the temple of God. The temple of God rises out of the singularity of consciousness, resurrecting the structures of immorality. Propelled by the power of light, the Son of God enters the dimensions of form. Pulsating revelations of light commune with the presence of God, opening form to the life of God. The living forms of light, energized by the power of God, expand, forming the infinite dimensions of light. The multidimensional realities of God are drawn inward toward the center of light, causing the dimensions of light to merge into singularities of thought. The thoughts of light lift into space, spinning free along the axis of God.

God is the fundamental reality of creation. The reality of God shapes the universe in the image of Himself. From the center of the created world the Son of God takes form. The formation of life begins with the word of everlasting light. The word of everlasting light is the celebration of God in the eternity of light. The eternity of light is the glorious ascension of everlasting splendor. From the splendor of the eternal Son the genesis of life takes form.

Life is the total potential of eternity inherent in the unity of God. The unity of God is the ever present center of existence. From the center of existence the eternal march of light proceeds into the life of God. The glory of God is revealed in the star of the ancient flame of eternity. The star of eternity is the material of light from the transcendence of God. The river of light flows in a steady stream of God's love into the creation of life.

The creation of life is the eternal continuum of the sacred knowledge of immortality. The knowledge of immortality is the internal mechanism of the Self-Illumined Light of God. The mechanism of immortality is revealed in the circle of the Self-Illumined Light of God. The mechanisms of light interaction are revealed in the Self-Illumined Light Body of God. They are the light networks that connect the twelve angelic essences of God.

The light networks of God form the grids of awareness, opening the awakening process of life. From the awakened light of God the forms of eternity merge into the splendor of life. The forms of eternity reveal the body of God. The body of God is the inherited gift from the source of life. It is the true offspring of God placed at the core of our being. The awakened body of God is the source of life in the age of light. The body of God is the material of life in the new age. The material of light is the substance of unity created to form structures of life. The new structures of life serve as the foundation of the new age of awakening splendor.

In the age of light all life will receive the full light of God. Life will use the material of light as its expression of love. The expressions of love are the inherited rights of the bodies of light. They are the sacred responsibility of the children of God. The children of God are the witness to the celebrated acts of God. The acts of God are the ancient stream of God's splendor flowing into the river of life. From the river of life God reveals His creations. The creations of God are the immortal lights of the sacred journey of life. The immortal lights of God are the life forms of the new age. The forms of light are the mechanisms of experience in the unity of God.

The mechanisms of experience are the conscious forms of God. The conscious forms of God exist in a stream of light flowing out from the ocean of love. The ocean of love is the source of all created life. It is the primordial form of life. From the primordial ocean of love the created lights of God reveal the body of God. They form the network of lights radiating out from the body of God. The network of lights are the combinations of the twelve angelic essences of God. The combinations of light structures flow out from a single light. The single light of God is the thread that binds the structures of light. The binding light of God is the unification of life. From a single thread of light the universe of God is born. The universe of God is the conscious relationships in the body of God.

The coming of light is revealed by the star of eternity. The star of eternity is the flame of immortality descending on wings of love. Descending on wings of love the white flame of God cleanses the earth with splendor. The splendor of God lifts humankind into the unification of light. The unification of light represents the total reality of God. It is the ancient call of light, revealing humanities origin in the body of God. The body of God is the eternal song of life. The eternal song of life lifts humankind to the pinnacle of truth in the unification of God. It frees the soul to live its full potential in the Self-Illumined Light of God.

The full potential of life is revealed in the unification of God. Life is the sacred gift of immortality from the source of light. From the ancient light of God the infinite source of life is resurrected in the life of humankind. The ring of light is the connecting guide of God. The connecting guide of God is the single thread of light translating the will of God to the children of light. From the ring of light the will of God administrates the Age of the Rising Sun. The Age of the Rising

Sun is the birth of God in the dimension of the transmutation of light. From the dimension of light the rising Son of God lifts humankind to the unification of life in God. The unification of life is the intelligence directing the administration of the ring of light. The connecting points along the ring of light receive the translations of light from the language of the Self-Illumined Light of God. The language of light is built from the fabric of eternal life. From the center of eternity the sacred awakenings of God form the fundamental building blocks of the ring of light.

The building blocks of light structure the movement of the ring of light in the body of God. The movement of light generates the evolution of life in the Self-Illumined Light of God. The evolution of life is the merging of light into the Self-Illumined Light Body of God. From the eternal song of life the angels of God carry the translated verses of light to the ring of light. From the ring of light verses of God are seeded into the bodies of the children of God.

The eternal flame of God is the self-effulgent center of eternity. From the effulgence of life the flame of God is forever burning in the hearts of humankind. The radiant heart of God is the sole light of eternity guiding the path to immortality. From the center of the radiant heart of God the angels descend on a cloud of sacred rose petals. The sacred petals of the rose are the living light essences of God. They are the fragrances of living light in the body of God. Through the touch of living light, God reveals the splendor of eternal life. From the center of the sacred rose, God sees the infinite lights of eternity. In the spaces between the petals of light, God hears the sounds of eternity. With the merging of living light, God tastes the light of eternity.

The life of God is the full expression of the sacred rose petals of eternity. Each petal represents a star seed of God. The star seeds of light germinate the spaces of eternity. They seed the fields of God with the light of eternal life.

The legions of light represent the honor of God. With the sacred sword of light, God removes the veil of self deception. Released from the veil of deception the children of light ascend to the unification of life in God. The legions of light reveal the path to God. They honor the sacred sword of God. From the hand of God the sword of light penetrates the spaces of eternity. In the depth of God's being the sword of light releases the seeds of light in a field of splendor. In a stream of resplendent joy the beginning of life takes form. Light merges into life revealing the eternity of God.

The river of God's joy finds its way to the ocean of God's love. In the ocean of light God gives birth to the divine Son. Merging out from the center of joy the Son of life enters the house of God. The power of light lives at the center of human existence. It breathes life into the forms of eternity. From the heart of God the radiant Son of God is born. The merging body of God reveals the splendor of eternal life. The first breath of life is a gift from the eternal light of God. Blessed by the power of light the Son of God takes form. On wings of light the Son of God enters the creation of God. The spirit of God lifts creation into the ascension of light revealing the unification of consciousness.

The sacred light of God reveals the power of light. From the center of the creative fires of God, emerging in a flame of knowledge the Self-Illumined Light of God fills creation with the power of light. The power of light is the genesis of the formation of life. Reverberating in the eternal silence of God the power of light energizes the birth of life. From the embryonic light formations of God the language of the Self-Illumined Light of God directs the manifestation of life. Received into the white flame of God, embryos of light emerge into the creation of life. The first seeds of life enter the womb of life. In the womb of life, God creates the eternal lights that become the stars of eternity.

The radiant sun fills life with the material of light. It draws light into the energy of form. The form of God is generated from the sun power of light. The sun power of light is the awakened Son of God. The awakened Son of God is the source of the generation of light in the sun. From the center of the radiant sun, God sends light into the universe. The light of God seeds the universe with the star children of light. The children of light seed the universe with the light of God. The merging light of God is the sun-star of eternity.

The sun-star of eternity is the living light of God. From the unity of God the living light material of creation is released into the universe of light. The universe of light is the created reality of God. It lifts life into the unification of God. Living light is the manifestation of God in the universe of the living God. The living God of light is the eternal presence of the Son of God. The Son of God is forever present as the white flame of immortality. In the Age of the Rising Sun, God lifts humanity into the white flame of immortality. Cleansed in the white flame of God the children of light are received into the Kingdom of God.

The eternal flame of God burns forever in the heart of life. From the eternal center of light, God created the world and its form. Light emerged as life out of the primordial substance of living light. The formations of life received the breath of life from the source of life. From the flame of immortality, God lives in the life of the children of light.

The doorway of light is the temple of immortality in the Kingdom of God. The temple of immortality is the resurrected Son of God. The resurrection of life is the sacred passage found at the center of life. The sacred passage of God is visible to the children of light. It is located at the doorway of light in the sacred temple of immortality, waiting for the moment when the star of eternity reaches its full illumination.

The star of eternity has revealed the path to God. The path to God is open to the children of light. It is the opened door of salvation, lifting humanity into the ascension of God.

THE TESTAMENT OF THE SON OF GOD

I entered the sun and whispered the thoughts of an eternal celebration of the face of God. I opened the form of God. It was enshroud in the splendor of an ancient light. I lifted the veil of rapture protecting the seeds of the sanctified light. Finding the exalted presence of life, I awakened to the sons and daughters of the consecrated light of the form of God.

Opened by the fabric of time, I am expanded across the space of God. Penetrated by the touch of God, I am reborn into the manger of light. Formed by the presence of holy light, I am resurrected into the eternal continuum of divine grace.

The wind of time lifted the veil of the sun-star, awakening the Son of God in the presence of the spirit of matter. Encircling the sun-star, the Son of God whispers the sounds of the continuous stream of everlasting joy. The celebrating lights of the face of God enter the sounds of the eternal celebration of God.

The bells of the reverberating sun-star echoed across infinity as the jubilation of light. The sacred form of God appeared as the presence of the sacred unions of eternal life. Fixed at the center of light the unions of light rotate around the axis of the word of God.

Vibrating at the center of light the sound of God shatters the spaces of existence, forming the structures of the ascending streams of eternal life. Rising in a continuous expansion of light, the Son of God resurrects the structure of light. Manifesting out of the silent spaces of eternal love, the peace of God penetrates the heart of life. Rivers of light poured out of the mouth of God, forming the framework of the existence of God. Manifesting sounds of light resurrected the eternal structures of God that live forever in the heart of the Son of God. In the divine spaces of the heart of God, the Son lives forever. I am the living testament of His presence. I reveal the mystery of His life. I hear the song of His heart. I am the resurrection of His light.

I am the witness to the great event of eternity. I record the great transformation into the Age of the Rising Sun. I form the universe of the great society of light. I reveal the mind of the creator of life. I deliver the keys that unlock the mechanisms of manifestation. I open the door to the eternal truth of God. I receive the creations of the great legions of light beings. I create the sounds of the eternal forms of God. I seed the nations of the great tribes of light. I enter The New Jerusalem of Light.

The New Jerusalem of Light

Love   The one hundred forty-four thousand children of light assembled in a sea of divine love.

Peace   The tapestry of the Self-Illumined Light of God's peace was created from threads of divine love.

Light   The connecting events of the Self-Illumined Light of God form the fabric of the light of God.

Joy   The union of divine light was born into the sacred space of the Self-Illumined Light of God.

Creation   The New Jerusalem of Light was created from the

Self-Illumined Light Body of God.

Truth	The consciousness of God is the material of The New Jerusalem of Light.
Radiance	An infinite space of light in a continuum of divine consciousness was born.
Illumination	A star of divine light emanates from the center of Her seven sacred pools of divine consciousness.
Beyond	The consciousness of light becomes the material for manifesting The New Jerusalem of Light.
Unity	We are the material of consciousness that gives birth to The New Jerusalem of Light.

I restore the ancient civilizations of light. I resurrect the ancient principles of God. I explore the forms of eternity as they unfold in the consciousness of light. I evolve the great nations of the indigenous races of God. I organize the consciousness of the one hundred forty-four thousand children of light. I build the material of light. I transform humanity into the form of God. I give birth to a new order of evolution. I raise the dead. I heal the sick. I walk the earth. I am the only begotten Son of the Father. Follow the internal inspirations that lead you to me. Leave the external world of false images. Join the legions of souls that walk with me. I am the way. I am the truth. I am the resurrected Son of God, transfigured in the white flame of God. I fulfill the destiny of light.

Created in the image of God the children of light inherit the life of God. Born from the ocean of everlasting joy, the Son of God descends into the peace of eternal life. Eternal life lifts the children of light into the sanctuary of God. The sanctuary of God is the light of the eternal sun radiating from the silence of the sacred thought. The sacred thought is the radiant Son of God, born from the union of light and love. The union of light and love is the embryo of truth created from the seed of eternal knowledge. The seed of eternal knowledge is the sacred word of God. The sacred word of God is the eternal presence of everlasting joy. Everlasting joy manifests as the continuum of light centered in the eternity of God. The eternity of God is the continuous flow of truth in the ocean of being. The ocean of being is the silence of God in the eternity of existence. Existence is the presence of light centered in a continuum of self-awakening. Self-awakening consciousness manifests truth as the eternal reality of God. The reality of God is the internal mechanism of self-awakening light. Self-awakening light is the creation of immortality in the union of existence. The union of existence is the invincible nature of light. The invincible nature of light is the self-generating mechanism of truth. Truth is the awakened light of eternity centered in the infinite existence of God. The infinite existence of God is the continuous manifestation of truth forming the fabric of eternal life. Eternal life organizes truth into the body of God. The body of God is the self-reflecting mechanism of consciousness. Consciousness guides light in the direction of immortality. Immortality is the continuous flow of self-reflecting consciousness expanding into eternity. The expanding light of God lifts the children of light into the life of God.

The life of God is the source of unlimited power and strength. Rising from the ocean of eternal love, the Son of God reveals the life of God. The life of God is the manifestation of truth forming a spiral of ever-unfolding realities of God. The realities of God form the universal light orders of intelligence. Orders of intelligence guide the formation of life in the body of God. The body of God organizes life into functional realities, specializing in the transmutation of light. The transmutation of light is the invisible force of God, manifesting into form. The manifesting forms of God reveal the eternal nature of existence. The eternal nature of existence guides life in the direction of immortality. Immortality is the self-generating mechanism of conscious realities manifesting into form. Manifesting realities of conscious beings form the universal orders of intelligence responsible for the administration of life. Administrators of light guide the formations of evolving intelligences in the body of God. The body of God receives the awakening lights into the womb of eternity. The womb of eternity releases the seeds of eternal life to the ocean of awakening love. Awakening love fills eternity with the splendor of existence. The splendor of existence is the creative force of self-generating light.

Self-generating light embraces the love of God with the fire of eternal knowledge. Eternal knowledge creates the mechanism for manifesting truth into form. The manifestation of truth is the sacred act of revelation giving birth to the body of God. The Body of God expands in a continuous stream of opening light filling space with the illumination of God. The illumined light of God represents the structure of eternity in the infinite spaces of silence.

The journey of light begins at the center of existence. Born from the impulse to awaken, existence reveals itself as the genesis of life. Life unfolds the journey back to the center of light. The center of light returns life to the source of existence. The source of existence is the guiding reality of light. Light administrates the awakening of life. Life awakens to the reverberations of light. Light reverberates at the center of existence. The center of existence reveals the nature of light. The nature of light is the sequential manifestation of the center of light. The center of light connects life to the center of existence. The center of existence frees life into the oneness of eternity. Eternity is the awakened light of existence centered in a continuous stream of love. Love unites light and existence in the creation of form. Form is the synthesis of light, love and existence. Existence is the binding reality of form, creating unlimited possibilities of expression. Expression unites love and light in the dance of life. Life embraces existence in the creation of form. Form guides life in the direction of immortality. Immortality is the self-sustaining reality of life. Life is the river of light, forever creating itself as the eternal presence of love. Love finds fulfillment in the journey of Light.

Released into the river of light, the children of eternity find their way into the ocean of everlasting joy. Everlasting joy receives life in the form of eternal expressions of light. Light is the continuous flow of consciousness reverberating in the spaces of eternity. Eternity awakens as the Son of Eternal Life. Eternal life calls the children of light into the unification of consciousness. Consciousness binds light in the form of eternal expressions of life. Life reveals light as the continuous flow of consciousness. From the sacred spaces of light, the universe reveals the formation of life. Life is the revelation of light in the form of eternal expressions of love. Love fills life with the many possibilities of self-awakening forms of light. Light is the eternal child of consciousness, forever manifesting itself as the ocean of everlasting joy.

Joy guides the children of light into the sun of eternal truth. Eternal truth reveals the recorded inscriptions of light written by the ancients of life. The ancients of life are the non-individual structures of consciousness residing in the spaces of eternity. The spaces of eternity are the realms of existence, centered in the mind of infinite light. The mind of infinite light is the organization of intelligence responsible for the structures of eternal truth. The structures of eternal truth are the non-visible realities of consciousness responsible for the administration of form.

The journey of light will find fulfillment in the year of the transmutation of light, transforming consciousness into the unification of light in God. The unification of light will reveal the transcendence of God as the reality of life. The reality of life is given by God to the children of light. The children of light will inherit the full reality of God. The reality of God is the transcendental existence of eternal life. Transcendence is the unified reality of consciousness lived at the heart of life. Created from light the universe reveals the journey back to God.

The signs of tomorrow guide the children of light into the final hour. The revelation of the final hour is delivered by the Son of God. The evolution of life culminates in the sun-star of eternity, forming the genesis of a new order of existence. The order of the Son of God is revealed by the revelations of the sacred unions formed at the center of light. The sacred unions of light enter the spaces of the sun-star, merging with the culminating life streams of the children of light. Forming light-unions of exploding realities of God, the new forces of life expand, filling space with the power of love.

In this planetary space the Son of Light takes his seat on the throne of God. Created from the inception of light, and born from the ancient consciousness, the Son of God reveals the entrance to the Kingdom of God. The entrance of light opens the salvation of God to the children of the eternal light of existence. The eternal light of existence fulfills the sacred promise of God given to the children of light. The children of light are the chosen receptacles of the holy light of existence. The holy light of God invites the children of the sacred word of God into the ocean of being.

Do you believe in the sacrament of light? I deliver life to the dead, peace to the broken hearted and light to the sanctified. I comfort the soul and release the spirit. Do not worry over the moments of living. Touch them with the assumption of light.

Here my prayer, I am the presence of God. Feel my love, I am the sanctuary of life. Accept my peace, it is the essence of God.

I emanate the forces of the divinity of God. Vakara is the force of eternity that structures the light of God into the tissues of life. Vasar is the love of God present in the tissues of life. Varna is the life force of God found in the tissues of life. Vasukra is the symmetry of light forming the relationships of the tissues of life.

Vasaya is the spring of light that forms the vessels of eternal life. Whoever receives the breath of God into the vessels of eternal life shall be transformed into the living light of God. Whoever breaths the living material of light will be resurrected in the heart of God.

Beloved is the life that stands before God. Humility is the gift that rises out of the hands of God. Peace is the reconciliation of light in the form of God. The form of God is the inner reality of the children of God.

In a place of solitude beyond the dimensions of space are the sacred realities of God. Above the mind and resurrected in the heart are the sacred formations of eternal life.

The witness of God reveals the final journey described by the ancients as the fire of living light. Transformed in the fire of living light, the final journey ascends to the living material of light. The ascent of the final journey reveals the nature of God. The nature of God is the material of light. Touched by the nature of God the witness of God is transfigured into the resurrected Son of God.

In the love of God we open our hearts to the inspiration of light. In the form of humanity, we open our thoughts to the presence of God. We are now free to create in the image of light.

We lift our hearts to divine inspiration. We release into the infinity of light. We reach out to the sacred joy resting in the quiet places of our hearts.

We are called by God to the sacred reality of light. We listen to the voice of God caressing our thoughts with visions of light. We are welcomed by the legions of angels into the ascended realities of light.

The Kingdom of God is the resurrected Son of God. Formed from the conception of light, the resurrected Son of God is transfigured into the Age of the Rising Sun. The Age of the Rising Sun is formed from the quarters of space and organized by the sequences of time. The sequences of time are characterized by the pulsating rhythms of spatial reality. Reality is the constituent form of God, created from the essence of light. The essence of light is captured by the intention of God to reveal the nature of his existence. The existence of God is the first cause of creation, opening space to the sequences of manifestation. The sequences of manifestation pulsate, dividing space into linear forms of light. The linear forms of light represent the ages of God. The ages of God are: the Age of the First Sun, the Age of the Rising Sun and the Age of the Last Sun. The Age of the First Sun is the birth of consciousness, the Age of the Rising Sun is the Son of God and the Age of the Last Sun is the liberation of light. The forms of God complete the cycles of time, liberating the sequences of light into the eternity of God. The sequences of light pulsate in harmony with the will of God. Manifested from sound, the sequences of light bifurcate into changing rates of vibration. The vibrations of light collapse space into a series of moments, creating linear reality in the form of past, present and future events. The events of light tell the story of the birth, resurrection and ascension of God. The story of light is witnessed by the children of God and celebrated in the Kingdom of God.

THE TWELVE TRANSFORMATIONS OF THE HOLY LIGHT OF GOD

The ancient records of transformation reveal the sequential expansion of the journey of light. The ancient records of light are descriptions of the transformation of matter into light. Light transformation occurs in twelve stages. The stages of transformation are: purity, splendor, love, peace, light, joy, creation, truth, radiance, illumination, beyond and unity. The twelve stages of transformation are the sacred awakenings of the Self-Illumined Light of God. They reveal the life of God at the center of existence.

The Scroll of Light

The Scroll of Light represents the ascent to God. The ascent of light is the material form of consciousness, rising from the ocean of being. The rising children of light ascend in a chorus of song. The song of eternity echoes the voice of God. The voice of God responds in rivers of awakening splendor. The splendor of light lifts the children of God into the ascending stream of awakening light. The awakening of God is recorded in the scroll of light. The scroll of light records the transmissions of the star seeds of God. The star seeds of light are the awakening memories of eternity sustained by the love of God. The memories of light form the arrangement of conscious realities of God. The realities of God descend into the spaces of eternity, filling silence with the manifestations of light. The silent forms of eternity open the dimensions of light, forming portals that pulsate light into material form. The portals of light reveal the ascending streams of eternity. The ascending streams manifest the material of God, forming multidimensional realities that connect consciousness to the absolute reality of God. The absolute reality of God reveals the cognition of the Son of God. The cognition of the Son of God is the scroll of the infinite light of God. The scroll of eternity fills the spaces of God with the memory of the absolute reality of God. The memory of light is the ascending stream of God, awakening life to the cognition of the absolute reality of God.

The Body of Light

The Body of Light is the genesis of a new evolutionary state of existence. Evolutionary states are a culmination of merging eternities combining into singularities of multi-cellular organisms. The singularities of life form units of specialized functions. Specialized functions translate invisible laws of light into form. The translations of light form the embryonic patterns administrating the development of multi-cellular organisms. Organisms of light expand in the eternity of space. The evolving light forms create living light material folding into patterns of ever-changing form and function. Changing patterns of light cause a cascade of reflecting images projected into space. The projected images of light receive the breath of life. The breath of life is the self-generating light of God. The self-generating light of God fills the universe with primordial structures of self-replicating intelligence. Self-replicating intelligence builds the embryonic body of light. The embryonic body of light is the self-sustaining organism responsible for the birth of light bodies.

Bodies of light combine in the eternity of space manifesting multi-cellular organisms of light. Organisms of light exist in a balanced state of unity suspended in a sphere of self-aware consciousness. Consciousness administrates the forms of light, causing an eternal expansion of vibrating light energizing the manifestation of God. The manifestation of God is the sacred event of light given by grace to the children of God.

The Messiahs of God

The Messiahs of God form the legions of incarnating realities of God. The realities of God manifest the continuous steam of ascending light. The stream of ascending light opens the forms of consciousness to the creations of light. The creations of light transform consciousness into living light. The transformation of consciousness is recorded in the scroll of light. The scroll of light receives consciousness, inverting the sequences of manifestation into the forms of God. The forms of God are resurrected from the inverting sequences of consciousness. Consciousness creates a vacuum in space, causing reality to collapse inward, forming physical space. Physical space organizes reality into multidimensional forms of ever changing design and function. The changing forms of God reveal the infinity of space, opening consciousness to the absolute reality of God.

The Unveiling of Light

Light is unveiled in the rapture of God. The rapture of God is poured into the vessels of eternal life. Eternal life opens the rapture of God to the children of the circle of the Self-Illumined Light of God. The children of light form the divisions of the circle of God. The circle of God vibrates in the eternity of space, forming the body of God. The body of God is activated by the grids of infinity, formed from the rapture of light.

The Form of Light

The Form of Light is the continuous correlation of events that take place within the context of the unification of light. The unification of light is the generator of events that reveal the nature of light. The nature of light is the manifestation of sequential unfolding realities of light. Realities of light form the context of expanding states of consciousness. The expansion of consciousness occurs within the framework of related events. Related events of light form structures of living material. The material of light is the fabric of consciousness, created from the sequences of unfolding realities of light. The sequential expansions of light form layers of self-interacting mechanisms that manifest The Form of Light.

The Encoded Sequences of Light

The Encoded Sequences of Light reveal the manifestation of God. Encoded in the arrangement of unfolding realities of light, are the sacred keys of immortality. The keys of light trigger cascading sequences of light revealing the patterns of intelligence that guide the ascension of God. The ascending lights of God are the encoded sequences of light. Recorded in the strands of light are the sequential expansions of the sounds of God. The sounds of eternity echo in the infinite spaces of light. The emanations of reverberating light reflect consciousness into conscious realities of form. Form organizes patterns of light, magnifying invisible laws of light. The magnification of light is the physical manifestation of energy patterns formed from the invisibility of light. The invisible nature of light unfolds the eternal patterns of consciousness, responsible for the existence of creation. Creation emerged from the forces of light, created out of the consciousness of God. Consciousness manifests the light of God into forms of conscious beings. Conscious realities of light manifest living material into form. The form of God expands in the infinite spaces of light. Consciousness enters the body of light. The body of light pulsates with the expanding consciousness of form. The form of eternity lifts into the ascension of God.

The Transformation into God

In the presence of God and the angelic kingdoms of light, the children of the Self-Illumined Light of God are resurrected as the ascending stream of totality. The ascending stream of totality lifts the children of God into the rapture of light. The rapture of light opens the language of God to the consciousness of form. The consciousness of form inverts, causing the center of light to open, giving birth to the universe of God.

The Created Lights of God

The lights of eternity create from the power of light. The invisible nature of light expands into the spaces of God. The power of God gives birth to the laws of light, creating the universe of God. The universe of God expands into the infinite dimensions of eternity forming the portals of light. The portals of light cause light and energy to exchange consciousness, creating light-energy conversion. Light-energy conversion manifests the body of God, filling life with the holy presence of God. The holy light of eternity lifts humankind into the ascension of God. The ascended lights of eternity take their place in the oneness of God. The one reality of God fills eternity with the totality of light.

The Mechanisms of Light

The Mechanisms of Light reveal the nature of manifestation in the body of light. The body of light is created out of the self-interacting mechanisms of light. Mechanisms of light reveal the recorded sequences of transformations in the body of light. Transformations occur in twenty-seven stages. The stages of light are: purity, splendor, love, peace, light, joy, creation, truth, radiance, illumination, beyond, unity, rapture, ecstasy, faith, compassion, effulgence, hope, power, eternity, wholeness, resplendence, oneness, dawn, bliss, strength and perfection. They represent the language of light. The language of light administers the awakening consciousness in the body of God. The awakening of consciousness is the opening of sequential unfolding realities of light. Realities of light form the arrangement of conscious events in the body of God. The body of God opens the transcendence

The Exploding Realities of God

The Exploding Realities of God form an invincible shield of consciousness, releasing swords of light into the spaces of eternity. The swords of light represent the power of God to penetrate the veils of illusion. The veils of illusion are the deceptions of consciousness formed from the concepts of reality. The concepts of reality are created from the perception of consciousness. The perception of consciousness is formed from the duel nature of light and love. Love invokes light opening a portal to the reality of God. The reality of God opens the field of consciousness, forming a vacuum in space. The vacuum of light opens a stream of ascending light, creating forms of awakening consciousness. The awakening light transcends the forms of consciousness, filling space with the reality of God.

The Revelations of Light

The Revelations of Light are responsible for the purification of consciousness. Consciousness moves in a continuous stream of expanding light. The expansion of light records the unfolding reality of light as encoded sequences in crystalline form. The crystalline forms of light manifest as internal structures of consciousness. The structures of light guide the awakening form of eternity. The revelations of light unveil the events of God, creating images of splendor. Moving in the ether of God, the Son of eternity opens the light of infinity, generating light centered conscious realities of God. Descending into form, the radiant Son of eternity delivers the encoded sequences of light to the children of the manifesting forms of God. Manifested forms of eternity reveal the nature of light. The nature of existence lifts consciousness into ascending realities of light. The ascending realities of light form a continuous stream of unfolding revelations of light. Moving in the context of light centered conscious realities, the Son of God reveals the commandments of God. The commandments of God form the body of laws responsible for the growth and maintenance of the body of light. They are administrated by the Self-Illumined Light of God. The administration of light is governed by the revelations of life. Revelations occur in twenty-seven stages of awakening. They are:

purity, splendor, love, peace, light, joy, creation, truth, radiance, illumination, beyond, unity, rapture, ecstasy, faith, compassion, effulgence, hope, power, eternity, wholeness, resplendence, oneness, dawn, bliss, strength and perfection.

The Corridor of Light

The Corridor of Light is the opening of consciousness, created from the arrangement of conscious realities of light. Realities of light form the framework for merging creations of truth. Truth manifests in the form of non-individual unions of self-generating light-energy. Light-energy crystallizes along an invisible grid of intersecting unions of consciousness. Unions of conscious beings administrate the flow of awakening creation in the form of transcendental images of light. Images of light guide the infusion of conscious realities with the inward flow of awareness. Awareness receives the conscious realities of light into the ocean of eternal truth. The ocean of truth opens its light, creating a bridge between the light of eternity and the material of unity. Material consciousness binds light in the form of unions of transcendental realities. Transcendental reality is the intelligence framework, guiding the manifestation of truth. Truth is the revelation of unions of self-aware realities of light.

THE TRANS·PORTAL MATRIX OF DIVINE GRACE

The transformation of light is recorded in The Trans-portal Matrix of Divine Grace. Trans-states intersect at the junction points where light-matter conversions produce dimensional portals wrapping space-time into a singularity. Consciousness transports along the singularity of space-time, traversing dimensionality in quantum bursts of radiant light. Expanded by inter-dimensional shifting, consciousness incorporates transformation into its existence.

The Trans-portal Matrix of Divine Grace is the ancient pathway revealed by God as the opening to light. The opening to light is the transmutation of consciousness from the limitation of matter to the infinite light of God. The infinite light of God manifests the pathway of light. The pathway of light opens the door to immortality. Immortality releases consciousness to the eternal light of God. The eternal light of God receives consciousness into the infinite consciousness at the source of life. The infinite consciousness reveals light as the truth of life. The truth of life is the power of transformation revealed by God as the power of light. The power of light is the manifestation of God in the form of eternity. The form of eternity is the immortal consciousness of awakening intelligence. The immortal consciousness of awakening intelligence structures light formations in the eternity of space. The eternity of space opens the pathway of light in the silence of consciousness. The silence of consciousness reveals the portals of light.

Centered in eternity The Trans-portal Matrix of Divine Grace opens consciousness to itself as the source of life. The opening of light transforms consciousness into the form of eternity. The form of eternity expands consciousness into the body of God. The body of God receives consciousness in the form of immortality. The form of immortality creates light from truth. The truth of God is expressed as the body of light in the form of eternity. Created from light the Son of God awakens in the eternity of space.

The Trans-portal Matrix of Divine Grace exists in the spaces of light, formed from the opening of silence in the heart of God. The heart of God is the center of light, created from the inception of form in the consciousness of God. The consciousness of God is the awareness of light, manifested from the sacred awakenings revealed by the cognition of light. The cognition of light is the resurrection of the I Am of God. The I Am of God is resurrected as the Son of the Eternal Flame of Immortality. Immortality is the form of God sustained by eternal love. Eternal love lives forever in the heart of God. The heart of God is the indwelling presence of the order of God. The order of God forms the invisible laws of light, responsible for the manifestation of God. The manifestation of God is revealed as the powers of light. The powers of light are generated from the personal cognitions of the children of light. The children of light organize the cognitions of God into radiant forms of life. The forms of life transform matter into material expressions of light. The expressions of light celebrate the existence of God. The existence of God expands, filling life with infinite forms of energy and intelligence. The forms of intelligence find expression in the consciousness of the children of light. The children of light witness the expanding forms of God, created by the cognitions of intelligence. The cognitions of intelligence are recorded in the ancient forms of eternity. The forms of eternity are the revelations of God, witnessed by the ancient life at the center of existence. The ancient light of God reverberates in the forms of eternity, awakening life to the infinite possibilities of God.

The Trans-portal Matrix of Divine Grace is recorded in the translations of light witnessed by the ancients of eternal life. The recorded translations of light are the sight and sound functions of the intelligence of immortality. Sight and sound form the holographic patterns of immortality. The immortality of light forms the nature of eternal life. Eternal life creates light from within the fabric of consciousness. Consciousness reveals God at the center of existence. The center of existence is the self-reflecting organization of intelligence. The self-reflecting organization of intelligence structures eternal life. Eternal life is the hope of humankind and the salvation of life.

Light rainbows connect the rays of God to the children of light. They release light crystals in the form of holographic patterns of intelligence. The holographic patterns represent the structures of eternal life. The structures of eternal life form a network of connecting patterns of light. The patterns of light reveal the body of God. The body of God represents the creations of God in the eternity of space and time. Space and time form the field of light interaction in the body of God. Light interactions are conscious connections of truth revealed by the children of light. The conscious connections of truth form the living light material of God. The material of light is expressed in shapes designed by God. The shapes of light reveal the splendor of eternal life. Eternal life expresses itself in the shapes of eternity. The shapes of eternity form the tapestry of living consciousness connecting the children of light in the eternity of God.

The shapes of eternity are the holographic images of light formed from the symmetry of life. The symmetry of life connects the images of form to the eternity of God. Form organizes light into creations of infinite order and intelligence. Creations of intelligence form conscious relationships of light symmetries in holographic form. The forms of light represent twelve divisions of light symmetries creating the circle of light. The circle of light is the basic structure of consciousness. It is the organization of light in the silence of eternity. The circle of light is the source of the shapes of eternity.

The twelve divisions of light symmetries in the circle of light are: purity, splendor, love, peace, light, joy, creation, truth, radiance, illumination, beyond and unity. The twelve light symmetries form the basic structure of all forms of living light. Forms of living light manifest images of unity into the splendor of creation. The splendor of creation receives the forms of light and generates shapes of ten sided holograms. The holograms of light fill eternity with the body of God. The body of God organizes the light formations into functional unions. The unions of light create reflections of eternity in the form of crystals of ever-changing form and function. The crystals of light initiate the ascension of consciousness in the creation of God.

The twelve crystals of light correspond to twelve expressions of God:

Purity	The Crown of God
Splendor	The Throne of God
Love	The Kingdom of God
Peace	The Son of God
Light	The Universe of God
Joy	The Birth of God
Creation	The Tapestry of God
Truth	The Power of God
Radiance	The Eternity of God
Illumination	The Omniscience of God
Beyond	The Transcendence of God
Unity	The Foundation of God

Within each expression of God are twelve crystals of light representing purity through unity. The light crystal of purity aligns the consciousness with the crown of God. The Crown of God restores the balance of light in the body of the child of light.

Splendor raises the frequencies of consciousness to the throne of God. The throne of God lifts consciousness to the ascension of God. The crystal of love fills consciousness with the Kingdom of God. The Kingdom of God expands consciousness into the creation of God. Peace restores clarity to the mind. The Son of God heals the life of the children of light. The crystal of light reveals The universe of God. The universe of God connects consciousness with the eternity of light. Joy opens consciousness to the birth of immortality. The birth of God delivers consciousness to the universe of light. Creation forms the connections of consciousness in the manifestation of light. The manifestation of light reveals the tapestry of God. The crystal of truth penetrates the veil of illusion, revealing the power of God. The power of God energizes consciousness into the many possibilities of God. Radiance generates unions of rays of light from The eternity of God. The eternity of God radiates consciousness from the light of God. The crystal of illumination awakens unity in the child of light. The omniscience of God fills eternity with the light of God. Transcendence reveals eternity as the source of light. The transcendence of God opens the door to eternal life. The crystal of unity binds consciousness in the eternity of God. The foundation of God reveals the unification of consciousness at the source of life.

The unification of consciousness is the living material of light. It is created from the spring of everlasting joy. The spring of joy is centered in a sea of liquid light. Liquid light flows into a vortex of opposing forces that combine to create a centripetal pull towards the center of light. The center of light expands upward in a series of circular progressions culminating in a symphony of color, sound, fragrance, texture and shape. The fountain of light creates a spring of life-giving light material. Light material is formed from the opposing forces of centripetal and centrifugal pulls, causing the suspension of liquid light in the form of material life. Material life is created from the arrangement of sequential unfolding spirals of rotating light formations. Light formations are built from the combining forces of gravity oscillating in a vortex of centripetal and centrifugal forces. The opposing forces suspend particles of light in a solution of floating gaseous material. The floating material of light rises in a chorus of celestial sounds. Celestial sounds reverberate in the spaces created from the rotation of living light material. Light material echoes the reverberations of sound, causing light energy to build forming spirals of illuminating centers spinning in space. The spinning centers of light form bodies of light rotating in harmony with the pulse of life. The pulse of life fills space with the celebration of light.

Living light celebrates its creation by generating images of awakening bursts of solar life-forms. Solar life is the spontaneous creation of light formations spinning in space. The spinning formations of light curve space creating a funnel, drawing light energy into form. Life forms within the energy matrix of light. The energy matrix of light contains the geometric patterns responsible for the formation of life. Life forms through the crystallization of metabolic forces within a solid state of existence. Metabolic forces combine to form energy matrices linked in cylindrical formations building living lattices that rotate in sequential progressions of living material. Living material is the culmination of layered sequences of increasing complexity moving in harmony with the pulsating bursts of solar life.

Created from pulsating bursts of light, life is propelled into existence. The merging life-forms manifest within a field of illuminating centers forming a web of interconnecting links of light. The connecting links of light are the communication networks guiding the manifestation of life. Life manifests by translating energy patterns, within the network, into form. Energy patterns represent sequenced rotations bifurcating into specialized functions. The bifurcation of light replicates material form by reflecting images into space. The reflecting images of light form independent tasks guided by illuminating centers within the web of light. The web of light creates life by combining reflection with pulsation resulting in self-perpetuating images of light. Pulsating images of light collapse space into subatomic spins, pulling light into inverted sequences that rotate in space. The inverted sequences reverse their rotation as space normalizes from its collapsed state. The reverse rotation of light releases energy into space forming multiple displays of living material. Living material releases symmetrical patterns of light forming symbiotic relationships of light. The symmetry of light guides the movement of symbiotic activity relative to the pulsating images of light. The pulsations of light form symbiotic relationships that reflect holographic mechanisms, translating light into material reality. The holographic mechanisms are created from the internal rotation of light bending inward towards its center. The inward pull of light curves space into multifaceted reflections of the center of light. The reflecting facets mirror the center of light from different angles forming a mosaic of multicolored lights. The mosaic of light rotates in space refracting light into empty space. The refracted light breaks into fragments forming crystals of light. Crystals of light combine forming lattice structures layered in translucent sheets of transcendental material. The transcendental layers of light form dimensional shifts creating the illusion of form. Form is structured from shifting patterns of light spinning in opposite directions creating a centrifugal force pushing light into space. Light penetrates the fabric of space causing an explosion of light-energy conversion. The energy created by the conversion of light expands out crossing the dimensional layers of light. The cross sections of layers of light and expanding energy form a grid of intersecting light. The grid of light is the infrastructure of creation energizing light into material form. Material form pulsates with the breath of life forming pyramids of light. Pyramids of light generate light impulses forming a communications network connecting the grid. Grids of light form matrix inversions drawing light into the pyramids. The pyramids convert light into energy creating an intelligence framework of pulsating bursts of light. The bursts of light form visual representations of energy patterns within the network. The energy patterns are the sequential unfolding reflections of the center of light. Concentric circles of reflecting light pulsate into form creating images of the center of existence.

Images of light combine to form highly organized systems of intelligence. The organizations of intelligence reveal the sequences of unfolding realities of light. The sequences are recorded in strands of living material. The strands of light are composed of translucent layers of particles suspended in a gaseous solution of light-energy. Light-energy is the creative spark that ignites the solution of light, causing an exhilaration of particle light interaction. Particle light interaction is the exchange of motion in a stream of opposing forces. Light expands forming a vacuum in space. The vacuum contracts forming particles of inert material. The density of material form draws the expanding light into its center, causing an explosion of living light. Living light is created from the infusion of light into material existence. Material reality bonds with inverted light sequences, created from the contracting light. The light sequences contain encoded frames that describe the nature of existence. The nature of existence is self-replicating light sequences that expand into form. Light expands within the context of opposing forces combining to form living expressions of existence. Living light-forms organize reality by creating structures of infinite design and function. The designs of living light translate intelligence into multidimensional forms of light sequences rotating in space. The rotating light sequences refract images of sequential unfolding reflections of the center of light. The center of light generates the impulse of living material, causing cascades of living streams of light to pour into form. Streams of living light fill the spaces of existence with awakening creation. Creation is the sequential unfolding reality of light. The realities of light are the mechanisms of manifestation, guiding the expansion of the center of light. The center of light expands, generating multidimensional shifts of changing reality states of existence. Existence unfolds reality states by creating multiple versions of shifting light patterns. Light patterns represent the sequential unfolding realities of existence. Reality organizes light into images of spectacular beauty and design. Created from the infinite spaces of existence, light unfolds itself into highly organized systems of intelligence.

The portals of light are the connecting lights of God, forming tapestries of interrelating lights of God. The interrelating lights of God create unions of self-aware consciousness forming the fabric of life in the portals of light. The portals of light organize life into the unification of God. The unification of light is the internal reality of life in the portals of light. The internal reality of life is the sacred gift of light given to the children of God. The children of God are the chosen receptacles of the ancient knowledge of immortality. The ancient knowledge of immortality is the self-awakening mechanism of the circle of light. The circle of light is the opening of eternity in the portals of light. The portals of light are the sacred openings of light connecting rings of light. Rings of light form the network of inter-connecting pathways of light. Pathways of light reveal the Self-Illumined Light Body of God. The Self-Illumined Light Body of God is the manifestation of light in the forms of eternity. The forms of eternity are the immortal structures of self-generating living light. The generation of living light is the self-reflecting mechanism of the Self-Illumined Light of God. The Self-Illumined Light of God is the internal mechanism of truth, revealing the unification of God. The unification of God is the living material of light, creating networks of inter-connecting pathways of light. Pathways of light form the relationships of unity in the body of God. The body of God is the union of light in the eternity of space. The eternity of space invites the birth of the holy light of God. The resurrection of light is the gift from the infinite consciousness, centered in the eternity of God.

The portals of light live in the sun of everlasting joy. Created from love the portals of light are born from the eternal spring of splendor. The eternal spring of splendor fills space with the light of God. The light of God creates life from the river of light. The river of light flows from the eternity of God. The eternity of God fills life with the creations of light. The creations of light form the fundamental structures of unity. Structures of unity inform the eternity of space with the intelligence of light. The intelligence of light structures life with the material of light. The material of light is the self-generating substance of immortality. The self-generating substance of immortality guides life in the direction of eternity. Eternity is the call of light in the silence of God. The silence of God is the reality of life in the portals of light.

The circle of light is the fundamental structure of unity in the portals of light. The structure of unity is divided into twelve divisions of light. The light divisions are: purity, splendor, love, peace, light, joy, creation, truth, radiance, illumination, beyond and unity. They are the self-aware mechanisms of manifestation. The divisions of light manifest the material of God in the form of eternity. The form of eternity guides the formation of structures of light. Structures of light merge in the eternity of space, creating crystals of light. Crystals of light combine forming lattices of living light. Lattices of living light form creations of immortality, manifesting life in the body of God. The body of God is the form of eternity giving birth to the portals of Light.

The portals of light are born from the self-aware consciousness of the circle of light. The self-aware lights of God form the fundamental reality of the portals of light. The reality of light is the transcendence of God. The transcendence of God is the source of life in the portals of light. The portals of light are the manifestation of the transcendent light of God in the golden sun of eternity. The golden sun of eternity is the presence of everlasting love. Everlasting love generates material of light, creating the portals of light.

We are the self-aware lights of God, manifesting structures of light from the sun of everlasting joy. The sun of everlasting joy fills life with the many possibilities of God's light. From the infinite possibilities of light we create the city of everlasting joy. The city of everlasting joy is born from the eternal consciousness of God. The eternal consciousness of God lives at the center of life. The center of life is the internal reality at the source of awareness. The awareness of God is the internal opening of light at the center of consciousness. The center of consciousness is the sun of everlasting joy.

The sun of everlasting joy generates the material of light from the center of consciousness. Rising in a chorus of light, the body of God enters the portals of Light. The portals of light expands giving birth to the Son of God.

Build the portals of light from the sacred transformations of the living heart of God. Open your heart to the life of God. Transform the heart of life into the vessels of eternal love. We are the emissaries of His divine plan. It is our life that reveals the heart of God.

Portals of Light

The portal of purity represents the ascension of God, responsible for the helix of light.

The portal of splendor represents the thought of God, responsible for the glorification of light.

The portal of love represents the form of God, responsible for the unification of light.

The portal of peace represents the word of God, responsible for the nature of light.

The portal of light represents the will of God, responsible for the evolution of light.

The portal of joy represents the celebration of God, responsible for the harmony of light.

The portal of creation represents the manifestation of God, responsible for the structure of light.

The portal of truth represents The Power of God, responsible for the movement of light.

The portal of radiance represents The Eternity of God, responsible for the rays of light.

The portal of illumination represents The Omniscience of God, responsible for the images of light.

The portal of beyond represents The Transcendence of God, responsible for the clarity of light.

The portal of unity represents The Foundation of

God, responsible for the unification of light.

Sub-Portal Matrices of Light

The sub-portal matrix of purity represents The Crown of God, responsible for the structure of light.

The sub-portal matrix of splendor represents The Throne of God, responsible for the manifestation of light.

The sub-portal matrix of love represents The Kingdom of God, responsible for the form of light.

The sub-portal matrix of peace represents The Son of God, responsible for the presence of light.

The sub-portal matrix of light represents The Universe of God, responsible for the expansion of light.

The sub-portal matrix of joy represents The Birth of God, responsible for the genesis of light.

The sub-portal matrix of creation represents The Tapestry of God, responsible for the connections of light.

The sub-portal matrix of truth represents The Power of God, responsible for the movement of light.

The sub-portal matrix of radiance represents The Eternity of God, responsible for the rays of light.

The sub-portal matrix of illumination represents The Omniscience of God, responsible for the images of light.

The sub-portal matrix of beyond represents The Transcendence of God, responsible for the clarity of light.

The sub-portal matrix of unity represents The Foundation of God, responsible for the unification of light.

Sub-Portal Matrices of Silence

The sub-portal matrix of purity represents The Eye of God, responsible for the vision of God.

The sub-portal matrix of splendor represents The Ear of God, responsible for the sound of God.

The sub-portal matrix of love represents The Body of God, responsible for the substance of God.

The sub-portal matrix of peace represents The Mind of God, responsible for the connections of God.

The sub-portal matrix of light represents The Consciousness of God, responsible for the intuition of God.

The sub-portal matrix of joy represents The Love of God, responsible for the celebration of God.

The sub-portal matrix of creation represents The Touch of God, responsible for the combinations of God.

The sub-portal matrix of truth represents The Soul of God, responsible for the threads of God.

The sub-portal matrix of radiance represents The Heart of God, responsible for the feelings of God.

The sub-portal matrix of illumination represents The Thought of God, responsible for the imagination of God.

The sub-portal matrix of transcendence represents The Silence of God, responsible for the space of God.

The sub-portal matrix of unity represents The Feet

of God, responsible for the sequence of God.

The sub-portal matrix of rapture represents The Ascension of God, responsible for the direction of God.

The sub-portal matrix of ecstasy represents The Emotions of God, responsible for the symmetry of God.

The sub-portal matrix of faith represents The Intellect of God, responsible for the transcendence of God.

The sub-portal matrix of compassion represents The Essence of God, responsible for the movement of God.

The sub-portal matrix of effulgence represents The Sound of God, responsible for the vibration of God.

The sub-portal matrix of hope represents The Faith of God, responsible for the knowledge of God.

The sub-portal matrix of power represents The Truth of God, responsible for the transformation of God.

The sub-portal matrix of eternity represents The Face of God, responsible for the light of God.

The sub-portal matrix of wholeness represents The Space of God, responsible for the form of God.

The sub-portal matrix of resplendence represents The Sanctity of God, responsible for the order of God.

The sub-portal matrix of oneness represents The Unification of God, responsible for the order of God.

The sub-portal matrix of dawn represents The Portal of God, responsible for the opening of God.

The sub-portal matrix of bliss represents The Glorifcation of God, responsible for the surrender of God.

The sub-portal matrix of strength represents The Invincibility of God, responsible for the self-generation of God.

The sub-portal matrix of perfection represents The Totality of God, responsible for the completion of God.

Universes of Light

The universe of purity represents the fountain of everlasting love, responsible for the genesis of life.

The universe of splendor represents the crystals of light, responsible for the formation of life.

The universe of love represents the awakening of light, responsible for the structures of life.

The universe of peace represents the presence of light, responsible for the knowledge of life.

The universe of light represents the creation of light, responsible for the manifestation of life.

The universe of joy represents the celebration of light, responsible for the harmony of life.

The universe of creation represents the connections of light, responsible for the fabric of life.

The universe of truth represents the movement of light, responsible for the transformation of life.

The universe of radiance represents the structure of light, responsible for the form of life.

The universe of illumination represents the revelations of light, responsible for the evolution of life.

The universe of beyond represents the transcendence of light, responsible for the material of life.

The universe of unity represents the completion of light, responsible for the fulfillment of life.

The light of God is the life of the universe. The universe of God is the light of humankind. The light of humankind is the door of eternity. The door of eternity is the light of eternal life. The light of eternal life is the opened light of God. The opened light of God is the solar life of God. The solar life of God is the salvation of light. The salvation of light is the journey of love. The journey of love is the creation of God.

The creation of God is the life of the solar lights of God. The solar lights of God are the ancient souls of eternal light. The ancient souls of eternal light are the givers of life. The givers of life are the sacred sun-stars of eternity. The sun-stars of eternity are the awakened lights of God. The awakened lights of God are the solar rays of eternity. The solar rays of eternity are the light angels of God. The light angels of God are the one hundred forty-four thousand children of light. The one hundred forty-four thousand children of light are the sacred events of God. The sacred events of God are the self-awakening mechanisms of light. The self-awakening mechanisms of light are the immortal structures of light in the body of God. The body of God is the organization of intelligence responsible for the administration of light. The administration of light is the sacred work of the twelve dimensions of God.

THE DIMENSIONS OF LIGHT

The dimensions of light enter the creation of God at the point of eternal light. The point of eternal light is the portal of ascension, the opened light of God. The opened light of God is the entrance to the Kingdom of God. The Kingdom of God is the sacred event of light living at the center of consciousness. From the center of consciousness, the dimensions of light carry the kingdom of light to the children of God. The children of God enter The dimensions of light, causing the transformation of light. The transformation of light is the sacred event, given by God to the children of light. Manifested into form the dimensions of light enter into the consciousness of life. Rising from the ocean of being, the Son of God fills the dimensions of light with the power of God. The power of God lifts the dimensions of light into the eternity of space. The eternity of space receives the dimensions of light into the infinite consciousness of God. Created from light, the dimensions of light expand, unifying the children of God. The children of God form the legion of light races, created to fulfill the ancient promise of salvation. The ancient promise of salvation is the covenant of light, given to the children of God at the beginning of time. The beginning of time was the inception point of light. The inception point of light gathered the forces of God into the portal of ascension, manifesting The dimensions of Light.

The dimensions of light represent the twelve stages of ascension. The stages of ascension are: purity, splendor, love, peace, light, joy, creation, truth, radiance, illumination, beyond and unity. They are the living transformations of light, responsible for the events of God. The events of God are the sacred initiations of light. The initiations of light are the sacred awakenings in the circle of the Self-Illumined Light of God. The awakenings of light are the stages of ascension responsible for the manifestation of God. The manifestation of God is the continuous transformation of light giving birth to the body of God.

The dimension of purity reveals the opening to light. The opening to light is the portal of ascension. The portal of ascension organizes the cells of the ancient light of God into the body of light. The body of light receives the love of God from the dimension of splendor. The dimension of splendor lifts the body of light into the splendor of eternal life. The eternity of light opens the door of eternal life, expanding the truth of God into the stream of awakening creation. Awakening creation manifests into the body of God, generating the material of light. The dimension of love moves into the corridor of light, revealing the Kingdom of God. The Kingdom of God manifests as the Son of the Eternal Presence of Light. The dimension of peace guides the lights of eternity into the Kingdom of God. From the peace of God, light fills eternity with the consciousness of God. The dimension of light expands eternity into the spaces of God. The spaces of God celebrate the coming of the Lord. The dimension of joy fills the spaces of God with the rapture of light. The rapture of light merges eternity into the life of God. The dimension of creation administrates the birth of God. The birth of God is the organization of light manifesting into the body of God. The dimension of truth reveals the power of the awakening light of God. Light awakens to the consciousness of God. The dimension of radiance opens the light of God, filling the spaces of eternity with the presence of God. The eternal presence of light radiates the full glory of God. The dimension of illumination fills consciousness with the knowledge of God. The knowledge of light organizes consciousness in the body of God. The dimension of beyond opens the transcendent light of God in the eternity of space. The eternal reality of light manifests into the dimensions of form. The dimension of unity forms the foundation of light, manifesting the body of God. The body of God forms the structure of the age of light.

THE FORMS OF ASCENDING LIGHT

The forms of ascending light are the mechanisms of ascension. They manifest the ancient consciousness at the source of life awakening the connections of light governing eternal life. The forms of ascending light connect the individual to streams of awakening consciousness rising out of the reality of God. The manifesting streams of conscious realms of light form the bases of multidimensional existence. Multidimensional existence enters form aligning consciousness with material reality. The alignment of consciousness with material existence reconciles the spirit with the will of God. The forms of ascending light reconcile the child light with the ancient form of God at the center of light.

Name of God

Love   The name of God is the crown of light placed on the altar.

Peace   The altar of God is the light placed on the throne.

Light	The throne of God is the light placed on the kingdom.
Joy	The Kingdom of God is the light placed on the earth.
Creation	The earth of God is the light placed in the heart.
Truth	The heart of God is the light placed in the soul.
Radiance	The soul of God is the light placed in your life.
Illumination	The life of God is the light placed in your soul.
Beyond	The name of your soul is the light of God.
Unity	The God name for you is...

Living Light

Love	From the divine milk of the Holy Mother's breast, comes the sacred substance of life.
Peace	The sweet nectar of divine substance brings peace to the heart.
Light	The sacred nectar of the Holy Mother radiates the loving light of God.
Joy	The joyous substance nourishes the living light material of the body.
Creation	The creative living light material of the Holy Mother is the genesis of life.
Truth	An infinite source of living light exists at the center of life.

Radiance	The living light of God is the true eternal source of life.
Illumination	The true light of God is found in the living light material of life.
Beyond	The transcendental substance of light is the new material of life.
Unity	The living light material of God forms the foundational love of the Holy Mother.

Cross of Invincibility

Love	The cardinal light of God is the cross of invincibility.
Peace	The cross of invincibility brings peace and protection to the children of God.
Light	Open your light to the cross of invincibility; the eternal presence of God.
Joy	Open your joy to the cross of invincibility; the eternal presence of God.
Creation	Open your hands to the cross of invincibility; the eternal presence of God.
Truth	Open your being to the cross of invincibility; the eternal presence of God.
Radiance	Open your heart to the cross of invincibility; the eternal presence of God.
Illumination	Open your intellect to the cross of invincibility; the eternal presence of God.

Beyond	Open your splendor to the cross of invincibility; the eternal presence of God.
Unity	Open your unity to the cross of invincibility; the eternal presence of God.

Cone of Ascension

Love	The cone of ascension descends from the light of God to the darkness of matter.
Peace	The cone of ascension is an invitation from the light of God to the darkness of matter.
Light	The cone of ascension is the initiation from the light of God to the darkness of matter.
Joy	The cone of ascension is the joy from the light of God to the darkness of matter.
Creation	The cone of ascension is the bridge from the light of God to the darkness of matter.
Truth	The cone of ascension is the breath from the light of God to the darkness of matter.
Radiance	The cone of ascension is the radiance from the light of God to the darkness of matter.
Illumination	The cone of ascension is the illumination from the light of God to the darkness of matter.
Beyond	The cone of ascension is the splendor from the light of God to the darkness of matter.
Unity	The cone of ascension is the purity from the light of God to the darkness of matter.

Cone of Purity

Love   The cone of purity comes from the heart of the Self-Illumined Light of God.

Peace   The cone of purity comes from the mind of the Self-Illumined Light of God.

Light   The cone of purity comes from the light of the Self-Illumined Light of God.

Joy   The cone of purity comes from the joy of the Self-Illumined Light of God.

Creation   The cone of purity comes from the hands of the Self-Illumined Light of God.

Truth   The cone of purity comes from the truth of the Self-Illumined Light of God.

Radiance   The cone of purity comes from the love of the Self-Illumined Light of God.

Illumination   The cone of purity comes from the intellect of the Self-Illumined Light of God.

Beyond   The cone of purity comes from the transcendence of the Self-Illumined Light of God.

Unity   The cone of purity comes from the purity of the Self-Illumined Light of God.

The Universe of God

Love
: From the light of God the universe structures immortality.

Peace
: From the grace of God the universe structures immortality.

Light
: From the effulgence of God the universe structures immortality.

Joy
: From the joy of God the universe structures immortality.

Creation
: From the touch of God the universe structures immortality.

Truth
: From the power of God the universe structures immortality.

Radiance
: From the radiance of God the universe structures immortality.

Illumination
: From the illumination of God the universe structures immortality.

Beyond
: From the transcendence of God the universe structures immortality.

Unity
: From the unity of God the universe structures immortality.

Centered in the Self-Illumined Light of God

Love   From the center of the Self-Illumined Light of God
                is the center of life.

Peace   From the center of the Self-Illumined Light of God
                is the peace of life.

Light   From the center of the Self-Illumined Light of God
                is the universe of life.

Joy   From the center of the Self-Illumined Light of God
                is the joy of life.

Creation   From the center of the Self-Illumined Light of God
                is the embrace of life.

Truth   From the center of the Self-Illumined Light of God
                is the truth of life.

Radiance   From the center of the Self-Illumined Light of God
                is the radiance of life.

Illumination   From the center of the Self-Illumined Light of God
                is the illumination of life.

Beyond   From the center of the Self-Illumined Light of God
                is the transcendence of life.

Unity   From the center of the Self-Illumined Light of God
                is the unity of life.

The Portal of Ascension

Love   The portal of ascension lives at the center of light.

Peace   The center of light is the breath of eternity in the ocean of love.

Light   The ocean of love is the living light of God.

Joy   The living light of God ascends the throne of light.

Creation   The throne of light connects eternity to living light.

Truth   Living light pulsates in the portal of ascension.

Radiance   The light of God radiates love from the portal of ascension.

Illumination   Consciousness expands in the portal of ascension.

Beyond The portal of ascension releases transcendence into life.

Unity   The portal of ascension receives life into unity.

Follow the Self-Illumined Light of God

Love   Follow the love of the Self-Illumined Light of God.

Peace   Follow the peace of the Self-Illumined Light of God.

Light   Follow the inspiration of the Self-Illumined Light of God.

Joy	Follow the joy of the Self-Illumined Light of God.
Creation	Follow the touch of the Self-Illumined Light of God.
Truth	Follow the truth of the Self-Illumined Light of God.
Radiance	Follow the radiance of the Self-Illumined Light of God.
Illumination	Follow the illumination of the Self-Illumined Light of God.
Beyond	Follow the splendor of the Self-Illumined Light of God.
Unity	Follow the purity of the Self-Illumined Light of God.

The Power of the Self-Illumined Light of God

Love	From the power of the Self-Illumined Light of God is the power of life.
Peace	From the power of the Self-Illumined Light of God is the peace of life.
Light	From the power of the Self-Illumined Light of God is the creation of life.
Joy	From the power of the Self-Illumined Light of God is the joy of life.
Creation	From the power of the Self-Illumined Light of God is

the birth of life.

Truth   From the power of the Self-Illumined Light of God is
             the truth of life.

Radiance   From the power of the Self-Illumined Light of God is
             the radiance of life.

Illumination From the power of the Self-Illumined Light of God is
             the illumination of life.

Beyond   From the power of the Self-Illumined Light of God is
             the splendor of life.

Unity   From the power of the Self-Illumined Light of God is
             the purity of life.

The Self-Illumined Light Body of God

Love   My eyes are of the Self-Illumined Light Body of God.

Peace   My ears are of the Self-Illumined Light Body of God.

Light   My mind is of the Self-Illumined Light Body of God.

Joy   My heart is of the Self-Illumined Light Body of God.

Creation   My hands are of the Self-Illumined Light Body of
             God.

Truth   My intellect is of the Self-Illumined Light Body of
             God.

Radiance   My being is of the Self-Illumined Light Body of God.

Illumination	My thoughts are of the Self-Illumined Light Body of God.
Beyond	My feelings are of the Self-Illumined Light Body of God.
Unity	My vision is of the Self-Illumined Light Body of God.

Commandments of the Self-Illumined Light of God

Love	All experience is death, God is life.
Peace	All objects are death, God is life.
Light	The wages of sin are death, God is life.
Joy	The wages of force are death, God is life.
Creation	The crown of God is life, Satan is death.
Truth	The power of God is life, evil is death.
Radiance	The eternity of God is life, mortality is death.
Illumination	The omniscience of God is life, ignorance is death.
Beyond	The transcendence of God is life, material is death.
Unity	The unity of God is life, separation is death.

Immortality

Love
: With the love of faith, God reveals the door to immortality.

Peace
: With the peace of faith, God reveals the door to immortality.

Light
: With the light of faith, God reveals the door to immortality.

Joy
: With the joy of faith, God reveals the door to immortality.

Creation
: With the hands of faith, God reveals the door to immortality.

Truth
: With the truth of faith, God reveals the door to immortality.

Radiance
: With the radiance of faith, God reveals the door to immortality.

Illumination
: With the illumination of faith, God reveals the door to immortality.

Beyond
: With the splendor of faith, God reveals the door to immortality.

Unity
: With the purity of faith, God reveals the door to immortality.

Laws of Light

Love
: The laws of light form the fundamental values of life.

Peace	The laws of light form the principal stages of evolution.
Light	The laws of light form the fundamental fabrics of creation.
Joy	The laws of light form the inherent principles of life.
Creation	The laws of light form the material expression of God.
Truth	The laws of light form the principal divisions of manifestation.
Radiance	The laws of light form the principal rays of reflection.
Illumination	The laws of light form the inherent logic of discrimination.
Beyond	The laws of light form the inherent experience of transcendence.
Unity	The laws of light form the interconnecting threads of unity.

Inorganic Material

Love	The innate intelligence in the vibration of material expression is the life of God.
Peace	The innate substance in the vibration of material expression is the life of God.
Light	The innate consciousness in the vibration of

material expression is the life of God.

Joy	The innate joy in the vibration of material expression is the life of God.
Creation	The innate creativity in the vibration of material expression is the life of God.
Truth	The innate truth in the vibration of material expression is the life of God.
Radiance	The innate effulgence in the vibration of material expression is the life of God.
Illumination	The innate light in the vibration of material expression is the life of God.
Beyond	The innate splendor in the vibration of material expression is the life of God.
Unity	The innate purity in the vibration of material expression is the life of God.

The Flame of God

Love	The flame of God liberates life from experience.
Peace	The flame of God generates life from light.
Light	The flame of God releases life into eternity.
Joy	The flame of God reveals life from sound.
Creation	The flame of God awakens life from God.
Truth	The flame of God opens life to truth.

Radiance	The flame of God radiates life from existence.
Illumination	The flame of God illuminates life from love.
Beyond	The flame of God transforms life from transcendence.
Unity	The flame of God unifies life in God.

Transformed into Light

Love	The witness to truth is transformed into light.
Peace	The witness to peace is transformed into light.
Light	The witness to love is transformed into light.
Joy	The witness to joy is transformed into light.
Creation	The witness to transcendence is transformed into light.
Truth	The witness to silence is transformed into light.
Radiance	The witness to eternity is transformed into light.
Illumination	The witness to knowledge is transformed into light.
Beyond	The witness to splendor is transformed into light.
Unity	The witness to purity is transformed into light.

THE CIRCLE OF ASCENDING LIGHT

The Circle of Ascending Light is the union of light received from the eternal silence of God. They are the building blocks of light, revealing the life of God. The life of God is revealed in the unveiling of twelve angelic essences. The twelve angelic essences are: purity, splendor, love, peace, light, joy, truth, creation, radiance, illumination, beyond and unity.

Purity

Splendor

Love

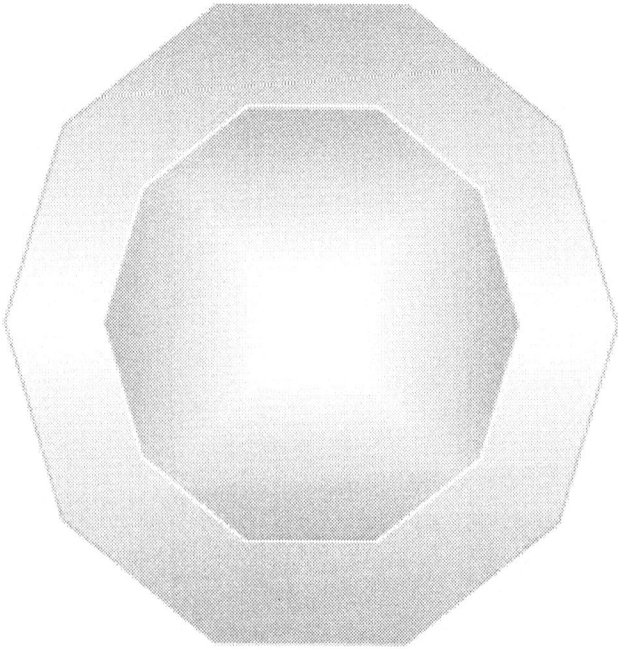

Peace

Light

Joy

Creation

Truth

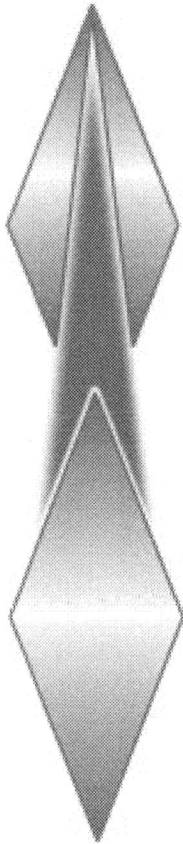

Radiance

Illumination

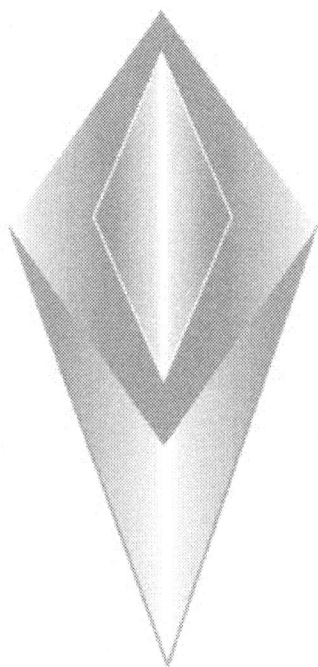

Beyond

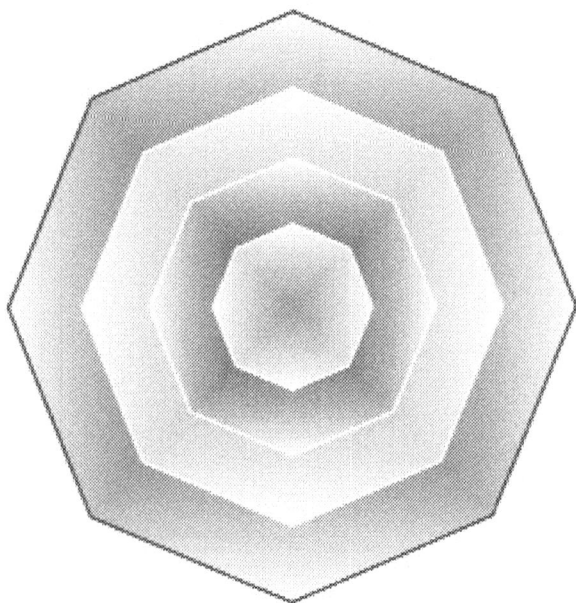

Unity

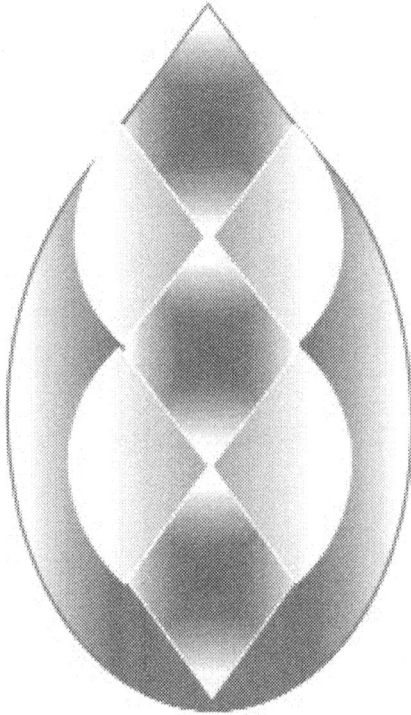

They form the fundamental divisions in the body of God. The twelve angelic essences are further divided to form the one hundred forty-four thousand children of God. The children of God are revealed in the verses of the twelve expressions of God. Each of the twelve expressions of God has a corresponding angelic essence. The expressions of God are divided into four books:

Book of Ascension

Purity	The Crown of God
Splendor	The Throne of God
Love	The Kingdom of God

Book of Healing

Peace	The Son of God
Light	The Universe of God
Joy	The Birth of God

Book of Meditation

Creation	The Tapestry of God
Truth	The Power of God
Radiance	The Eternity of God

Book of Enlightenment

Illumination	The Omniscience of God
Beyond -	The Transcendence of God
Unity	The Foundation of God

The twelve angelic essences form the circle of the Self-Illumined Light of God. The angelic essences manifest into the twelve expressions of God through the keys of the Self-Illumined Light of God. Each key is placed over an angelic essence in order to manifest its expression of God. The keys act as energy conduits, transmitting the light of God through the angelic essences of the circle of the Self-Illumined Light of God. The first manifestation is the crown of God from the angelic essence of purity. The crown of God is placed on the forehead inviting the helix of the Self-Illumined Light of God to enter the body. The helix of the Self-Illumined Light of God begins the process of transmutation of the physical body into the God material body of light.

The twelve angelic essences are found within each expression of God. For each angelic essence found in an expression of God there are ten verses. The ten verses represent love through unity. Purity and splendor are un-manifest and are expressed through beyond and unity. Splendor is expressed through beyond and purity through unity.

The verses of the twelve expressions of God invite a process called angelic integration shift high energy. This is the invitation into the circle of the Self-Illumined Light of God. The circle of light is the total expression of the nature of existence. It is the source of the infinite possibilities of the Creator. The act of love is the genesis of the creative power of the circle of the Self-Illumined Light of God. The creative power of light is the source of the life of angels. The angels of God are the administers of the high energy shift of the ascension process. The ascension process is the evolution of matter from the limitation of ignorance to the limitless possibilities of awareness. Awareness is the mechanism for revealing the truth of God. The circle of the Self-Illumined Light of God is the mechanism for the expansion of consciousness into awareness of the unification of life in God. The structures of Light initiate the angelic integration shift high energy process, transforming life through the Self-Illumined Light of God.

The Self-Illumined Light of God is the consciousness mechanism responsible for the ascension of life to the unification of consciousness in God. The consciousness of unification is the fundamental reality of ascension. It is the inherited life from the source of unlimited power in the Self-Illumined Light of God. From the center of the eternal spring of the seven sacred pools of consciousness the Self-Illumined Light of God radiates the truth of existence. The radiant truth of God resounds throughout creation lifting life to the unification of consciousness in God.

Unification is the living light material of God's presence in the dimension of love. The dimension of love is the sacred trust of God given to the souls of the ancient journey of life. The ancient journey of life is the growing recognition of the truth of God. It is born from the desire of God to know Itself as the source of all existence.

The circle of ascending light contains the inscriptions of the sacred trust of God given to the ancients of life eternal. The ancients of life are the chosen receptacles of the holy light of existence. They are the formations of the intelligence of existence. It is their light that guides the destiny of eternal life. The Brotherhood of Light form the fabric of possible incarnations of the Self-Illumined Light of God.

The incarnations of the Self-Illumined Light of God are the expansions of the ancients into the body of God. The body of God is the eternal expression of the sanctity of existence. It is the revelations of the sacred awakenings found in the circle of the Self-Illumined Light of God. The sacred awakenings of God occur in twelve stages. The twelve stages are purity, splendor, love, peace, light, joy, creation, truth, radiance, illumination, beyond and unity. The sacred awakenings of God manifest into the twelve angelic essences forming the circle of the Self-Illumined Light of God. The twelve angelic essences are the fundamental divisions in the body of God.

The twelve angelic essences reveal the sequential manifestation of the life of God. They describe the relationships in the body of God. They are the threads that bind the life of God to the body of God. It is their life that forms the foundation of the building blocks of creation. The building blocks of creation are an expression of the interplay of the life of God. They are the celebrated acts of the angels of God.

The angels of God form the structure of the light body of God. They are the network of communication pathways in the light body of God. It is their light that reveals the Self- Illumined Light Body of God. The Self-Illumined Light Body of God is the gift from the eternal light of God to the children of the sacred love of God. The children of God are the celebrated unions of the life of angels. They are the witness of the manifestation of eternity into the splendor of creation. They number one hundred and forty-four thousand, the exact number of angels in the body of God.

The angels pour their light into the embryonic pathways of the body of God. Emanations of sequential patterned lights guide the growth of the body of God. They form the intelligence of the interrelations found in the creation of the body of God. They are the order of language expressed in the silence of the sacred union of life. The language of light represents the sounds of the unions of eternity in the body of God. The sounds of the language of light are the creations of love expressed in the light body of God. The sounds of light are the manifestations of intelligence in the forms of the eternal expansion of God. They are the structures of knowledge governing the evolution of the body of God. The material of light is the life giving substance of the Holy Mother. The liquid light of God is the universal seed of eternity planted in the heart and mind of the Son of God.

The Self-Illumined Light of God is the organizing function of the Creator. It is the guiding light of God given to the people of the one spirit. The spirit of God is the unifying force of the inner reality of life. The forces of life come from the source of the eternal spring of love. They are the manifestations of the eternal silence of God. The order in the universe is the direct expression of the forces of God. The forces of God are the powers of light found in the life of angels. The circle of the Self-Illumined Light of God is the source of life in the universe. It is the creative force giving life to the body of God, illuminating all of existence. The emanations of light form the connecting structures in the body of God. The angels of God expand out from the center of the Self-Illumined Light of God. They form the administrating function of the Self-Illumined Light of God. They administer the will of God throughout the body of God. Their life is the music of the celestial spheres of God. The music of the spheres represents the harmonies of life. They form the connecting rhythms in the light body of God. The dance of angels is the connecting rhythms guiding the movement in the Self-Illumined Light of God. The movements in God provide the links connecting The Circle of Ascending Light in the body of God. The grids of light are the mechanisms of intelligence supporting the functions in the light body of God. The mechanisms of intelligence are the coexisting states of awareness in the Self-Illumined Light of God. The states of awareness are the evolving life forces in the body of God. They combine revealing the totality of consciousness in the eternity of existence. The nature of existence is continual expansion. The expansion of consciousness is the purpose of the Self-Illumined Light of God.

Consciousness is the knowing mechanism of the eternity of existence. It is the intelligence that guides the awakening in the Self-Illumined Light of God. The awakening of light is the joyous celebration in the body of God. It is the mission of light to awaken the children of God. The body of God is the field of light centered in the thought of eternity. The thought of eternity is the guiding will of the light of God. The will of God is the central focus in the body of God. The central focus is the truth of eternity expressed in the Self-Illumined Light of God. The truth of God radiates throughout the Self-Illumined Light Body of God. It is the manifestation of organizing power in the body of God. Organizing power is the mechanism of expansion in the body of God.

The fabrics of consciousness form the linking mechanism binding states of awareness in the Self-Illumined Light of God. The states of awareness are linked through a single thread of light in the body of God. The thread of light is the channel of eternal love from the source of infinite splendor. The created reality of God is the sanctioned life in the body of God. From a single thread of light to the grand multiplicity of light is the domain of the Self-Illumined Light of God. The multiplicity of light represents the universe of the Self-Illumined Light of God. The universe of God is the will of the Son of God. The Son of God is the sole created offspring of the body of God. The offspring of God is the birth of light on the plane of Aldrea. Aldrea is the golden child of immortality in the universe of the Self-Illumined Light of God. It is the embodiment of the eternity of God. The domain of Aldrea is the third and fourth dimensions of the Self-Illumined Light of God. These are the dimensions of the transmutation of light. The transmutation of light is the physical merging of the material of the Self-Illumined Light of God. God material is the true substance of the Self-Illumined Light Body of God. It is the physical reality of the unification in the Self-Illumined Light of God. The material of light is the personal consciousness of the Self-Illumined Light of God. The children of God are the offspring of the Self-Illumined Light of God. The material of light is the consciousness of the children of God. Consciousness is the guiding force in the body of God.

The guiding force of the Self-Illumined Light of God is the ancient flame of eternal light. The ancient flame describes the intelligence in the language of the Self-Illumined Light of God. The language of light is a sequence of unfolding awakening tones of light. The tones of light reverberate in the infinity of awakening splendor. They are the structures of eternity expressed through the verses of the Self-Illumined Light of God. The verses of the Self-Illumined Light of God represent the behavior in the body of God. The behavior of God is expressed in the relationships of the twelve divisions of the body of God. The twelve divisions of the body of God are: purity, splendor, love, peace, light, joy, creation, truth, radiance, illumination, beyond and unity. They are the fundamental building blocks of the grammar found in the language of the Self-Illumined Light of God. The grammar of light describes the linking mechanisms in the body of God. The linking mechanisms are the conscious relationships of the ancients of life. The ancients of life represent the desire of God to know Himself. The knowledge of light is revealed through the sacred awakenings in the body of God. The sacred awakenings of purity through unity are the twelve stages of enlightenment found in the Self-Illumined Light of God. Enlightenment is the self-realization experienced through the Self-Illumined Light of God. Self-realization is the mechanism of organization in the Self-Illumined Light of God. The organizations of light are the knowing mechanisms in the body of God. They are the celestial spheres representing the twelve states of awareness. Each sphere is a dimension of awareness in the Kingdom of God. The Kingdom of God is the eternal presence of wings of light kindled by the white flame of truth.

On golden rays of endless love, wings of light penetrated the sacred spheres of God. Kindled in the sacred fire of the white flame, the union of light was born. Resurrected in spheres of golden light, the awakened presence of eternity revealed the angels of God. The ancients of life are the angels of the sacred spheres of God. Angels are the personalized invitations from the ancient consciousness at the source of life. They are the instruments of divine revelation, setting in motion the sacred journey of light. The sacred journey of light is contained in the inscriptions from the golden seed at the basis of creation. The genesis of life originated from the golden seed of the eternal flame of God. The pure flame of God is forever radiating the love of God. God's love is the golden sun centered in a halo of resplendent purity. The golden sun is the source of immortality giving long life to the children of light. Rising in a chorus of celebration the children of light ascend through the sacred spheres of God entering the unification of consciousness.

The conscious expansion of the children of God is the organization of light in the spheres of the angels of God. The organization of light is the journey given by God to the children of light. This journey is the sanctioned life in the Self-Illumined Light Body of God. It is the source of symmetry in the body of God. The awakened lights of God fulfill the sacred promise given to the children of God. The sacred promise of God is the continual expansion of eternity in the spheres of awareness experienced by the children of God.

The twelve expressions of God form the sequential expansion of the ascension process. The ascension process unfolds the relationship of life in the body of God. It reveals the source of life in the Self-Illumined Light of God.

The crown of God is the first expression of God, and is experienced as purity in the Self-Illumined Light of God. Purity structures the basis of the ascension process. It links the helix of the Self-Illumined Light of God with the body of light placed in the earth body. The helix of light contains all mechanisms for transforming the earth body into the God material body of light. The body of light is the truth of eternal life in the Self-Illumined Light Body of God.

The ascension process further expands into the throne of God, lifting the earth body into the body of light. The body of light is placed on the throne of God. The throne of God is the seat of eternity in the house of God. The house of God is the domain of light in the splendor of eternity. The throne of God raises the frequencies of the earth body to match the light body of God. The light body of God carries the earth body to the throne of God. The throne of God anchors the earth body into the body of God.

The Kingdom of God connects the love of God to the children of God. From the Kingdom of God the earth body is expanded to embrace the totality of God's creation. God's creation represents the balance of life in the body of God. It is the love of God that binds the relationships of unity in the Self-Illumined Light of God.

The Son of God extends the light of God to the children of light. The children of light receive the peace of God from the light of salvation. The light of salvation releases love to the children of God. The children of God find fulfillment in the peace of God.

The universe of God fills the spaces of eternity with the lights of infinity. The lights of infinity expand life to the limitless possibilities of God. From the infinite possibilities of God, the children of light are revealed by the lights of infinity. The infinite lights of God are the children of the eternal expansion of God.

The birth of God releases the souls of God into the streams of ascending light. The souls of light form an embryonic fold in space gathering light in the form of God.

The tapestry of God draws the threads of light into material substance creating the garments of eternal life.

The power of God opens the portals of light filling space with the structures of light.

The eternity of God penetrates the vessels of life with the presence of God.

The omniscience of God awakens life to the body of God.

The transcendence of God opens life to the reality of God.

The foundation of God is the testament of light witnessed by the children of light.

The Crown of God
The Welcoming Spirit of Light

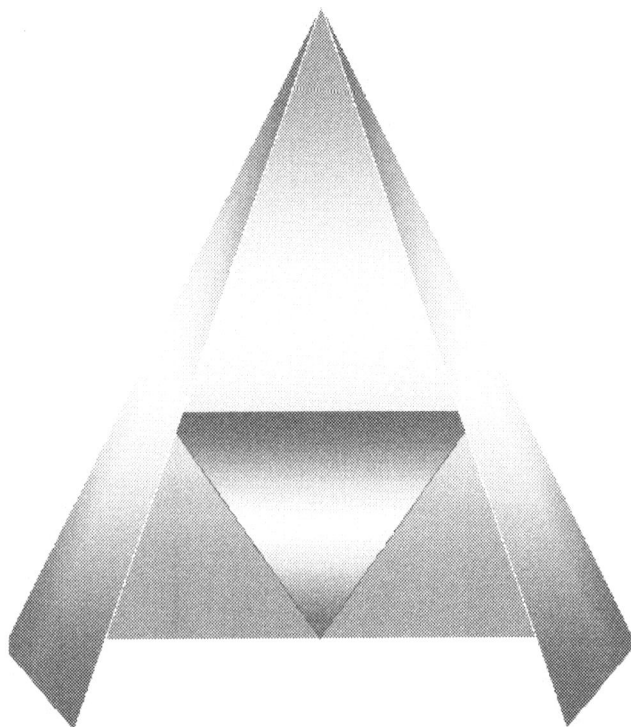

Love

Love	My soul is on fire with the love of God.
Peace	My heart is at peace with the passion of God.
Light	My eyes are illumined with the sight of the Lord.
Joy	My heart sings the songs of the Lord.
Creation	My ears hear the voice of the Lord.
Truth	My heart swells with each reverberating note.
Radiance	My hands touch the silence of God.
Illumination	My heart echoes the joy of the song.
Beyond	My mind knows the love of God.
Unity	My heart energizes the song of God.

Peace

Love	I am the source of peace, the eternal light.
Peace	I am the source of life, the peace of the world.
Light	I am the light of the world, the source of peace.
Joy	I am the creator of the world and its form.
Creation	I am life, the beginning and the end.

Truth	I am the beginning of life, the source of truth.
Radiance	I am the end of life, the source of light.
Illumination	I am the nations and the light of the world.
Beyond	I am the ocean where the rivers rest.
Unity	I am the rivers where the waters are free.

Light

Love	I am the body of light, the place of eternal love.
Peace	I create the bridge between the worlds of light and love.
Light	I am the light of God that guides the path of truth.
Joy	I place the flame on the altar of eternal life.
Creation	I sow the seeds of the eternal truth of light.
Truth	I am the store house of the eternal truth of life.
Radiance	I am the ambassador of the holy truths of eternal light.
Illumination	I am the messenger of the sacred heart of God.
Beyond	I am the stepping stone to the throne of His salvation.
Unity	I am the eternal one, the beginning of life and the fulfillment of love.

Joy

Love	I am the resurrection and the light.
Peace	I am the truth of the lamb.
Light	I am the beginning of life.
Joy	I conquer all fears.
Creation	I nourish all pain.
Truth	I feel all sorrow.
Radiance	I accept all light.
Illumination	I give all love.
Beyond	I bring the light.
Unity	I hear the song.

Creation

Love	I build the foundations of truth and the structures of love.
Peace	I remember the seeds I released upon the earth and the nourishment of the truth.
Light	I sowed the eternal truths of light in the seeds of life.
Joy	I harvest the spirit in the sun of truth and release the seeds to the womb of life.

Creation	I caress the child and attend the flock of the eternal Son.
Truth	I soothe the heart and cleanse the life of the lamb who blesses the world.
Radiance	I release the truth to the children of light so that they may radiate light.
Illumination	I receive the light and place its flame on the altar of truth.
Beyond	I bless the light and spread its holy presence upon the world.
Unity	I fulfill the sacred promises given to the children of light who walk upon the earth.

Truth

Love	I am the knower of truth and the Lord of love.
Peace	I am the bestower of peace and the master of truth.
Light	I am rejoicing in the truth of salvation.
Joy	I am spreading the truth on the fabric of life.
Creation	I am resurrecting the structures of eternal truth.
Truth	I am the Lord of truth and the light of the world.
Radiance	I sit on the throne of truth, radiating light.
Illumination	I imagine the truth and bear witness to the light.

Beyond	I am the truth, the light of the world.
Unity	I am the world, the manifestation of truth.

Radiance

Love	In truth all life is love.
Peace	In peace all love is truth.
Light	In light all truth is love.
Joy	I am the truth and the light.
Creation	I am the resurrection and the life.
Truth	I am the light of the world.
Radiance	I am the one who was there in the beginning.
Illumination	I am the one who is revealed in the end.
Beyond	I am the Son and the Father.
Unity	I am the lamb of God.

Illumination

Love	In the beginning there was love.
Peace	Peace spread upon the earth.
Light	Light illumined the skies.

Joy	The sacred joy had begun.
Creation	The journey of light was initiated.
Truth	The souls departed to the earth.
Radiance	The radiance came to cleanse the thoughts.
Illumination	The light came to awaken the souls.
Beyond	The Son came to gather His own.
Unity	The Lord embraced the children of light.

Beyond

Love	In the gap between light and love.
Peace	There exists the peace of divine love.
Light	In the light between space and time.
Joy	There exists the thought of divine light.
Creation	In the realm of space there is love.
Truth	In the realm of time there is light.
Radiance	In the light of God there is life.
Illumination	In the Son of life there is light.
Beyond	In the birth of God there is life.
Unity	In the life of God there is truth.

Unity

Love In the beginning of life the star seeds were spread upon the earth.

Peace The eternal light sowed the star seeds into the fabric of love.

Light The peace of the Lord gathered the light from the corners of the earth.

Joy The angelic hosts rejoiced with the coming of the Lord.

Creation The birth of the Lord had given form to the divine Son.

Truth The Son of truth gathered the star seeds into the heart of God.

Radiance In the manger of the Divine Mother the Self-Illumined Light of God was born.

Illumination The Self-Illumined Light of God was resurrected in the heart and in the mind of God.

Beyond The star seeds were gathered into the light of divine love.

Unity The unity of light was gathered into the peace of God.

Splendor

Love	We wish to express our love.
Peace	We are the life of God.
Light	We are the light of existence.
Joy	It is our joy to welcome you.
Creation	We are the brotherhood of creation.
Truth	It is the truth that we share.
Radiance	Our song is the harmony of life.
Illumination	Our life is the song of the Lord.
Beyond	Our love is the light of God.
Unity	Our God is the light of existence.

Purity

Love	I am the singularity of love.
Peace	I am the silent point of light.
Light	I am the light focused on the world.
Joy	I am the world focused on joy.
Creation	I created the world from the one.

Truth	This is the truth of the one life.
Radiance	This is the life of the one God.
Illumination	This is the truth of the one reality.
Beyond	This is the reality of God.
Unity	God is all that exists.

The Throne of God
The Guiding Principle of Light

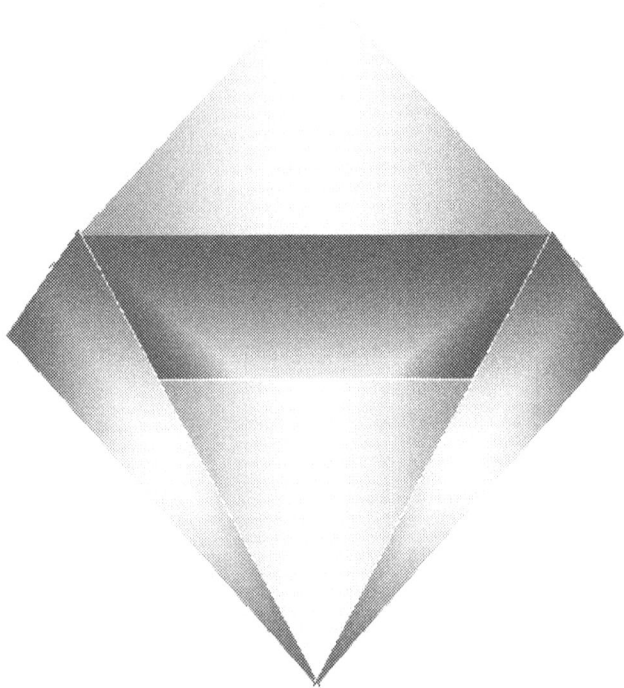

Love

Love	My love comes through the frequencies of space and time.
Peace	My peace comes through the frequencies of space and time.
Light	My light comes through the frequencies of space and time.
Joy	My joy comes through the frequencies of space and time.
Creation	My creation comes through the frequencies of space and time.
Truth	My truth comes through the frequencies of space and time.
Radiance	My radiance comes through the frequencies of space and time.
Illumination	My illumination comes through the frequencies of space and time.
Beyond	My transcendence comes through the frequencies of space and time.
Unity	My unity comes through the frequencies of space and time.

Peace

Love   We are the frequencies of love.

Peace   We are the frequencies of peace.

Light   We are the frequencies of light.

Joy   We are the frequencies of joy.

Creation   We are the frequencies of creation.

Truth   We are the frequencies of truth.

Radiance   We are the frequencies of radiance.

Illumination We are the frequencies of illumination.

Beyond   We are the frequencies of transcendence.

Unity   We are the frequencies of unity.

Light

Love   Light is the frequency of love.

Peace   Love is the frequency of peace.

Light   Peace is the frequency of light.

Joy   Light is the frequency of joy.

Creation   Joy is the frequency of creation.

Truth	Creation is the frequency of truth.
Radiance	Truth is the frequency of radiance.
Illumination	Radiance is the frequency of illumination.
Beyond	Illumination is the frequency of transcendence.
Unity	Transcendence is the frequency of unity.

Joy

Love	Joy raises the frequency of love.
Peace	Love raises the frequency of peace.
Light	Peace raises the frequency of light.
Joy	Light raises the frequency of joy.
Creation	Joy raises the frequency of creation.
Truth	Creation raises the frequency of truth.
Radiance	Truth raises the frequency of radiance.
Illumination	Radiance raises the frequency of illumination.
Beyond	Illumination raises the frequency of transcendence.
Unity	Transcendence raises the frequency of unity.

Creation

Love	Creation is the truth of love.
Peace	Love is the truth of peace.
Light	Peace is the truth of light.
Joy	Light is the truth of joy.
Creation	Joy is the truth of creation.
Truth	Creation is the truth of knowing.
Radiance	Knowledge is the truth of radiance.
Illumination	Radiance is the truth of illumination.
Beyond	Illumination is the truth of transcendence.
Unity	Transcendence is the truth of unity.

Truth

Love	Truth energizes the frequency of love.
Peace	Love energizes the frequency of peace.
Light	Peace energizes the frequency of light.
Joy	Light energizes the frequency of joy.
Creation	Joy energizes the frequency of creation.

Truth	Creation energizes the frequency of truth.
Radiance	Truth energizes the frequency of radiance.
Illumination	Radiance energizes the frequency of illumination.
Beyond	Illumination energizes the frequency of transcendence.
Unity	Transcendence energizes the frequency of unity.

Radiance

Love	I radiate the frequencies of light throughout all love.
Peace	I radiate the frequencies of love throughout all peace.
Light	I radiate the frequencies of peace throughout all light.
Joy	I radiate the frequencies of light throughout all joy.
Creation	I radiate the frequencies of joy throughout all creation.
Truth	I radiate the frequencies of creation throughout all knowing.
Radiance	I radiate the frequencies of knowing throughout all truth.
Illumination	I radiate the frequencies of truth throughout all illumination.
Beyond	I radiate the frequencies of illumination throughout all existence.
Unity	I radiate the frequencies of existence throughout all unity.

Illumination

Love	I illuminate the frequencies of love.
Peace	I illuminate the frequencies of peace.
Light	I illuminate the frequencies of light.
Joy	I illuminate the frequencies of joy.
Creation	I illuminate the frequencies of creation.
Truth	I illuminate the frequencies of truth.
Radiance	I illuminate the frequencies of radiance.
Illumination	I illuminate the frequencies of life.
Beyond	I illuminate the frequencies of transcendence.
Unity	I illuminate the frequencies of unity.

Beyond

Love	I breath transcendence into love.
Peace	I breath love into peace.
Light	I breath peace into light.
Joy	I breath light into joy.
Creation	I breath joy into creation.

Truth	I breath creativity into truth.
Radiance	I breath truth into radiance.
Illumination	I breath radiance into illumination.
Beyond	I breath illumination into transcendence.
Unity	I breath transcendence into unity.

Unity

Love	God is love.
Peace	Love is peace.
Light	Peace is light.
Joy	Light is joy.
Creation	Joy is creation.
Truth	Creation is truth.
Radiance	Truth is radiance.
Illumination	Radiance is illumination.
Beyond	Illumination is transcendence.
Unity	Transcendence is unity.

Splendor

Love	The splendor of God restores the frequencies of love.
Peace	The splendor of love restores the frequencies of peace.
Light	The splendor of peace restores the frequencies of light.
Joy	The splendor of light restores the frequencies of joy.
Creation	The splendor of joy restores the frequencies of creation.
Truth	The splendor of creation restores the frequencies of truth.
Radiance	The splendor of truth restores the frequencies of radiance.
Illumination	The splendor of radiance restores the frequencies illumination.
Beyond	The splendor of illumination restores the frequencies of transcendence.
Unity	The splendor of transcendence restores the frequencies of unity.

Purity

Love	Purity is the frequency of love.
Peace	Purity is the frequency of peace.

Light	Purity is the frequency of light.
Joy	Purity is the frequency of joy.
Creation	Purity is the frequency of creation.
Truth	Purity is the frequency of truth.
Radiance	Purity is the frequency of radiance.
Illumination	Purity is the frequency of illumination.
Beyond	Purity is the frequency of transcendence.
Unity	Purity is the frequency of unity.

The Kingdom of God
The Building Spirit of Light

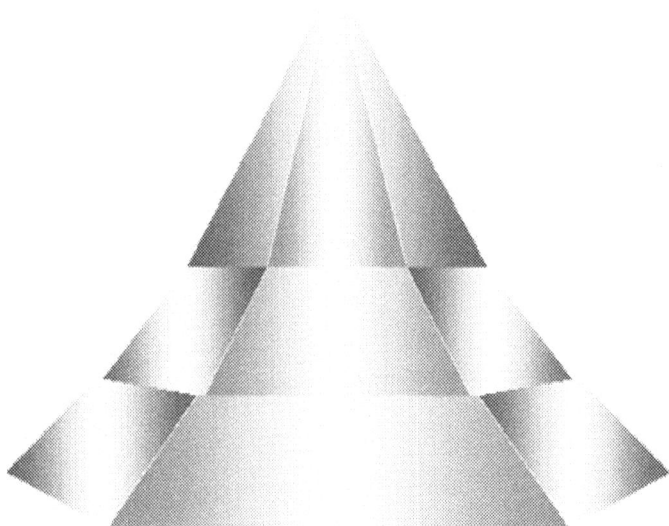

Love

Love	It is the blue white and gold world that I love.
Peace	It is in her oceans and streams that I play.
Light	It is in her forests where I dance with the angelic lights.
Joy	It is on her lands where I sing the songs of life.
Creation	It is through her love that I enjoy creative expression.
Truth	It is on her highest mountain that I see the Self-Illumined Light of God.
Radiance	It is from her deepest ocean that He radiates the strongest love.
Illumination	It is in her driest desert that He quenches the greatest thirst.
Beyond	It is under her softest rains that He comforts the gentlest heart.
Unity	It is in her love that the union is born.

Peace

Love	I give my love for the peace of the earth.
Peace	I give my peace for the light of the earth.
Light	I give my light for the joy of the earth.

Joy	I give my joy for the creation of the earth.
Creation	I give my creation for the truth of the earth.
Truth	I give my truth for the radiance of the earth.
Radiance	I give my radiance for the illumination of the earth.
Illumination	I give my illumination for the splendor of the earth.
Beyond	I give my splendor for the purity of the earth.
Unity	I give my purity for the unity of the earth.

Light

Love	With the sword of love I remove the darkness.
Peace	With the sword of peace I remove the darkness.
Light	With the sword of light I remove the darkness.
Joy	With the sword of joy I remove the darkness.
Creation	With the sword of creation I remove the darkness.
Truth	With the sword of truth I remove the darkness.
Radiance	With the sword of radiance I remove the darkness.
Illumination	With the sword of illumination I remove the darkness.
Beyond	With the sword of transcendence I remove the darkness.
Unity	With the sword of unity I remove the darkness.

Joy

Love	In the joy of love, the Holy Mother gives birth to the Self-Illumined Light of God.
Peace	In the joy of peace, the Holy Mother gives birth to the Self-Illumined Light of God.
Light	In the joy of light, the Holy Mother gives birth to the Self-Illumined Light of God.
Joy	In the joy of God, the Holy Mother gives birth to the Self-Illumined Light of God.
Creation	In the joy of creation, the Holy Mother gives birth to the Self-Illumined Light of God.
Truth	In the joy of truth, the Holy Mother gives birth to the Self-Illumined Light of God.
Radiance	In the joy of radiance, the Holy Mother gives birth to the Self-Illumined Light of God.
Illumination	In the joy of illumination, the Holy Mother gives birth to the Self-Illumined Light of God.
Beyond	In the joy of splendor, the Holy Mother gives birth to the Self-Illumined Light of God.
Unity	In the joy of purity, the Holy Mother gives birth to the Self-Illumined Light of God.

Creation

Love	I breath love into the Self-Illumined Light of God.
Peace	I breath peace into the Self-Illumined Light of God.
Light	I breath light into the Self-Illumined Light of God.
Joy	I breath joy into the Self-Illumined Light of God.
Creation	I breath life into the Self-Illumined Light of God.
Truth	I breath truth into the Self-Illumined Light of God.
Radiance	I breath radiance into the Self-Illumined Light of God.
Illumination	I breath illumination into the Self-Illumined Light of God.
Beyond	I breath transcendence into the Self-Illumined Light of God.
Unity	I breath unity into the Self-Illumined Light of God.

Truth

Love	The radiant truth seeds love on the earth.
Peace	The radiant truth seeds peace on the earth.
Light	The radiant truth seeds light on the earth.
Joy	The radiant truth seeds joy on the earth.

Creation	The radiant truth seeds healing on the earth.
Truth	The radiant truth seeds power on the earth.
Radiance	The radiant truth seeds eternity on the earth.
Illumination	The radiant truth seeds illumination on the earth.
Beyond	The radiant truth seeds splendor on the earth.
Unity	The radiant truth seeds purity on the earth.

Radiance

Love	In the radiant heart of the earth there is love.
Peace	In the radiant heart of the earth there is peace.
Light	In the radiant heart of the earth there is light.
Joy	In the radiant heart of the earth there is joy.
Creation	In the radiant heart of the earth there is healing.
Truth	In the radiant heart of the earth there is truth.
Radiance	In the radiant heart of the earth there is eternity.
Illumination	In the radiant heart of the earth there is illumination.
Beyond	In the radiant heart of the earth there is splendor.
Unity	In the radiant heart of the earth there is purity.

Illumination

Love   I am exhilarated with the touch of love.

Peace   I am exhilarated with the touch of peace.

Light   I am exhilarated with the touch of light.

Joy   I am exhilarated with the touch of joy.

Creation   I am exhilarated with the touch of healing.

Truth   I am exhilarated with the touch of power.

Radiance   I am exhilarated with the touch of eternity.

Illumination   I am exhilarated with the touch of illumination.

Beyond   I am exhilarated with the touch of splendor.

Unity   I am exhilarated with the touch of unity.

Beyond

Love   I weave a thread of splendor binding love to peace.

Peace   I weave a thread of splendor binding peace to light.

Light   I weave a thread of splendor binding light to joy.

Joy   I weave a thread of splendor binding joy to creation.

Creation   I weave a thread of splendor binding creation to truth.

Truth	I weave a thread of splendor binding truth to radiance.
Radiance	I weave a thread of splendor binding radiance to illumination.
Illumination	I weave a thread of splendor binding illumination to transcendence.
Beyond	I weave a thread of splendor binding transcendence to unity.
Unity	I weave a thread of splendor binding unity to purity.

———

Unity

Love	The purity of God is the foundation of love.
Peace	The purity of God is the foundation of peace.
Light	The purity of God is the foundation of light.
Joy	The purity of God is the foundation of joy.
Creation	The purity of God is the foundation of creation.
Truth	The purity of God is the foundation of truth.
Radiance	The purity of God is the foundation of radiance.
Illumination	The purity of God is the foundation of illumination.
Beyond	The purity of God is the foundation of splendor.
Unity	The purity of God is the foundation of unity.

Splendor

Love	I weave the threads of splendor into the fabric of love.
Peace	I weave the threads of splendor into the fabric of peace.
Light	I weave the threads of splendor into the fabric of light.
Joy	I weave the threads of splendor into the fabric of joy.
Creation	I weave the threads of splendor into the fabric of creation.
Truth	I weave the threads of splendor into the fabric of truth.
Radiance	I weave the threads of splendor into the fabric of radiance.
Illumination	I weave the threads of splendor into the fabric of illumination.
Beyond	I weave the threads of splendor into the fabric of transcendence.
Unity	I weave the threads of splendor into the fabric of unity.

Purity

Love	Rest in the purity of my love.

Peace	Rest in the purity of my peace.
Light	Rest in the purity of my light.
Joy	Rest in the purity of my joy.
Creation	Rest in the purity of my creation.
Truth	Rest in the purity of my truth.
Radiance	Rest in the purity of my radiance.
Illumination	Rest in the purity of my illumination.
Beyond	Rest in the purity of my splendor.
Unity	Rest in the purity of my unity.

The Son of God
The Redeeming Spirit of Light

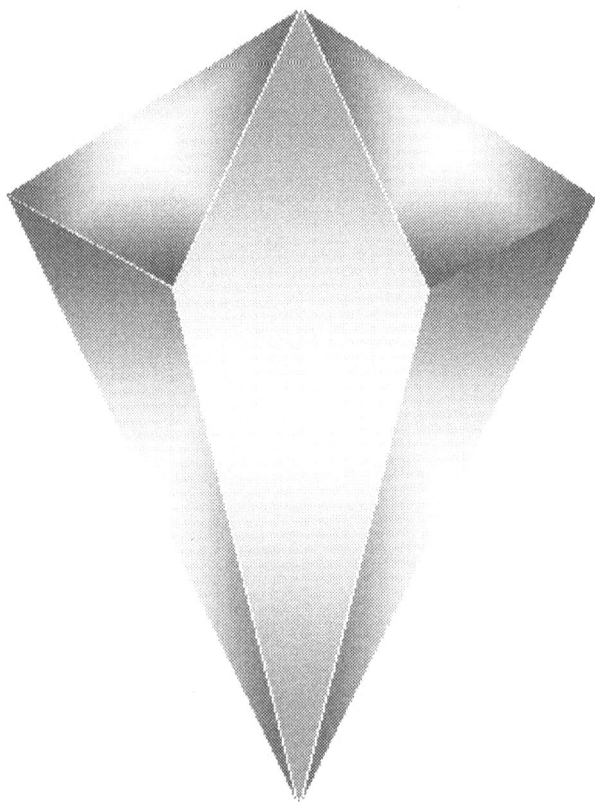

Love

Love	Let my love go deep into your heart.
Peace	Let my peace go deep into your being.
Light	Let my light go deep into your mind.
Joy	Let my joy go deep into your life.
Creation	Let my creation go deep into your thoughts.
Truth	Let my truth go deep into your light.
Radiance	Let my radiance go deep into your love.
Illumination	Let my illumination go deep into your peace.
Beyond	Let my transcendence go deep into your truth.
Unity	Let my unity go deep into your radiance.

Peace

Love	The peace of God's love surrounds you.
Peace	The peace of God's tranquility surrounds you.
Light	The peace of God's light surrounds you.
Joy	The peace of God's joy surrounds you.
Creation	The peace of God's creation surrounds you.

Truth	The peace of God's truth surrounds you.
Radiance	The peace of God's radiance surrounds you.
Illumination	The peace of God's illumination surrounds you.
Beyond	The peace of God's transcendence surrounds you.
Unity	The peace of God's unity surrounds you.

Light

Love	I am the light of God, eternal love.
Peace	I am the light of God, eternal peace.
Light	I am the light of God, eternal life.
Joy	I am the light of God, eternal joy.
Creation	I am the light of God, eternal strength.
Truth	I am the light of God, eternal truth.
Radiance	I am the light of God, eternal radiance.
Illumination	I am the light of God, eternal illumination.
Beyond	I am the light of God, eternal splendor.
Unity	I am the light of God, eternal unity.

Joy

Love   The sacred heart of joy is a gift of love.

Peace   The sacred heart of joy is a gift of peace.

Light   The sacred heart of joy is a gift of light.

Joy   The sacred heart of joy is a gift of life

Creation   The sacred heart of joy is a gift of creation.

Truth   The sacred heart of joy is a gift of truth.

Radiance   The sacred heart of joy is a gift of radiance.

Illumination   The sacred heart of joy is a gift of illumination.

Beyond   The sacred heart of joy is a gift of transcendence.

Unity   The sacred heart of joy is a gift of unity.

Creation

Love   Let my creation embrace you with love.

Peace   Let my creation embrace you with peace.

Light   Let my creation embrace you with light.

Joy   Let my creation embrace you with joy.

Creation   Let my creation embrace you with life.

Truth	Let my creation embrace you with truth.
Radiance	Let my creation embrace you with radiance.
Illumination	Let my creation embrace you with illumination.
Beyond	Let my creation embrace you with splendor.
Unity	Let my creation embrace you with purity.

Truth

Love	Truth is the awakening of love.
Peace	Truth is the awakening of peace.
Light	Truth is the awakening of light.
Joy	Truth is the awakening of joy.
Creation	Truth is the awakening of creation.
Truth	Truth is the awakening of life.
Radiance	Truth is the awakening of radiance.
Illumination	Truth is the awakening of illumination.
Beyond	Truth is the awakening of transcendence.
Unity	Truth is the awakening of unity.

Radiance

Love	The radiant Son of God is love.
Peace	The radiant Son of God is peace.
Light	The radiant Son of God is light.
Joy	The radiant Son of God is joy.
Creation	The radiant Son of God is born.
Truth	The radiant Son of God is truth.
Radiance	The radiant Son of God is eternity.
Illumination	The radiant Son of God is illumination.
Beyond	The radiant Son of God is transcendence.
Unity	The radiant Son of God is unity.

Illumination

Love	The light of forever is the Kingdom of God.
Peace	The light of forever is the Son of God.
Light	The light of forever is the universe of God.
Joy	The light of forever is the birth of God.
Creation	The light of forever is the tapestry of God.

Truth	The light of forever is the power of God.
Radiance	The light of forever is the eternity of God.
Illumination	The light of forever is the omniscience of God.
Beyond	The light of forever is the transcendence of God.
Unity	The light of forever is the unity of God.

Beyond

Love	I place myself in clear silent love.
Peace	I place myself in clear silent peace.
Light	I place myself in clear silent light.
Joy	I place myself in clear silent joy.
Creation	I place myself in clear silent creation.
Truth	I place myself in clear silent truth.
Radiance	I place myself in clear silent radiance.
Illumination	I place myself in clear silent illumination.
Beyond	I place myself in clear silent transcendence.
Unity	I place myself in clear silent unity.

Unity

Love	The song of God bridges the space between love and peace.
Peace	The song of God bridges the space between peace and light.
Light	The song of God bridges the space between light and joy.
Joy	The song of God bridges the space between joy and creation.
Creation	The song of God bridges the space between creation and truth.
Truth	The song of God bridges the space between truth and radiance.
Radianc	The song of God bridges the space between radiance and illumination.
Illumination	The song of God bridges the space between illumination and transcendence.
Beyond	The song of God bridges the space between transcendence and unity.
Unity	The song of God bridges the space between unity and God.

Splendor

Love	I release to the transcendence of love.
Peace	I release to the transcendence of peace.
Light	I release to the transcendence of light.
Joy	I release to the transcendence of joy.
Creation	I release to the transcendence of creation.
Truth	I release to the transcendence of truth.
Radiance	I release to the transcendence of radiance.
Illumination	I release to the transcendence of illumination.
Beyond	I release to the transcendence of splendor.
Unity	I release to the transcendence of unity.

Purity

Love	Before thought, there existed a pure state of love.
Peace	Before thought, there existed a pure state of peace.
Light	Before thought, there existed a pure state of light.
Joy	Before thought, there existed a pure state of joy.
Creation	Before thought, there existed a pure state of creation.

Truth	Before thought, there existed a pure state of truth.
Radiance	Before thought, there existed a pure state of radiance.
Illumination	Before thought, there existed a pure state of illumination.
Beyond	Before thought, there existed a pure state of transcendence.
Unity	Before thought, there existed a pure state of unity.

The Universe of God
The Infinite Dimensions of Light

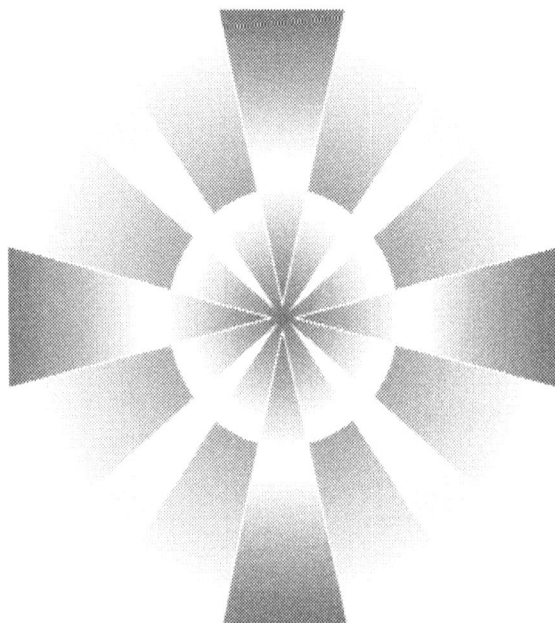

Love

Love	Exploding white light surrounding a vast space centered in love,
Peace	The gathering of light into the center of peace in the love of God,
Light	The spreading of love upon the infinite rays of divine light in the heart of God,
Joy	The praising of God is the joyous celebration in the universe of light.
Creation	The birth of God is the blessing of love from the eternity of life.
Truth	The fire of creation purifies the way of divine truth on the path of life.
Radiance	The radiant light of an infinitude of beings across the universe of God,
Illumination	The illumined Seraphim of divine light invite all to share in the holy birth of God,
Beyond	The transcendent light of holy love is the resurrection of the eternal now,
Unity	The unity of all light in the Lord is the blessing of God.

Peace

Love   In the gentlest place in your heart, the Lord is born.

Peace   In the largest space of your heart, the Self-Illumined Light of God is resurrected.

Light   From the radiant light of God's heart, the Son has come to take His throne.

Joy   In this planetary space, the Holy Mother has given birth to a new order of life.

Creation   A new order of creation takes up the commandments of God.

Truth   The true light ascends to the crown of God from the throne of the Self-Illumined Light of God.

Radiance   The Self-Illumined Light of God radiates out from the center of the Kingdom of God.

Illumination   The awakening of life in the new order weaves a tapestry of peace.

Beyond   The connecting threads of silent love awaken the transcendent splendor of God.

Unity   From silent point to silent point, the one reality can be found everywhere.

Light

Love
The seven sacred pools of divine consciousness are centered in a radiant stream of light.

Peace
The serenity of the sacred pools of the Self-Illumined Light of God brings peace to all who will open their heart.

Light
The sanctification of life comes from the seed of the Self-Illumined Light of God.

Joy
The sphere of joy that constitutes the sacred pools of life is the Self-Illumined Light Body of God.

Creation
The birth of God is the joyous celebration of the Seraphim of Light.

Truth
The connecting lights of the Self-Illumined Light Body of God form the reality of the new earth.

Radiance
From a single point of light a new commandment radiates on the earth.

Illumination
It is the voice of the alpha and the omega, the beginning and the end.

Beyond
It is the hand of the Self-Illumined Light of God reaching down from the love of God.

Unity
It is the raising up of the children of light to the crown of God.

Joy

Love	Let the trumpets of joy sound for all to hear.
Peace	Let the peace makers stand up and be heard.
Light	Let the one hundred forty-four thousand children of light go into the nations.
Joy	May the jubilation of the Lord be felt in all hearts.
Creation	May the birth of the new order be known to all people.
Truth	May the truth of God be the salvation of your life.
Radianc	May your heart radiate the love of the Self-Illumined Light of God.
Illumination	May your mind be illumined with the Self-Illumined Light of God.
Beyond	May your light merge with the Self-Illumined Light of God.
Unity	May your light rest in the purity of God.

Creation

Love	The eternal reality of God breaks through the physical reality of creation.
Peace	The inner space of deep silence is the ocean of eternal existence.

Light	The eternal light of God radiates from the altar of eternal life.
Joy	The birth of life comes from the spring of eternal joy.
Creation	The eternal reality of God spins around a center of light, manifesting the universe into existence.
Truth	The expanding light builds a bridge in the eternity of space, connecting truth to all of existence.
Radiance	The messages of truth radiate out from the center of the expanding light of God.
Illumination	The Self-Illumined Light of God proceeds out from the center of God's holy light.
Beyond	The splendor of the Self-Illumined Light of God gives purpose to the angelic hosts who administer God's divine plane.
Unity	The wheel of connecting divine light rotates around a central point of purity.

Truth

Love	A multitude of beings carry the light of God.
Peace	They rest in a sea of resplendent light contemplating the truth of God.
Light	They are focused on a single point of light, the place of eternal truth.
Joy	The revelation of divine truth kindles the eternal celebration of the Lord.

Creation	The creative spark of effulgent light fills the void with the truth of the Self-Illumined Light of God.
Truth	The radiant light of God penetrates deep into the truth of the existence of eternal life.
Radiance	The revelation of the eternal light of God exploded into one hundred forty-four thousand rays of light.
Illumination	The illumined rays of God form the Self-Illumined Light Body of God.
Beyond	The transcendence of God is the truth of the rays of the Self-Illumined Light Body of God.
Unity	The Self-illumined rays of God weave a tapestry of unity in the body of God.

Radiance

Love	The radiant light of the Son of God is the opened door of salvation.
Peace	All are welcome in the light of forever, the eternal presence of the Lord.
Light	The doorway to light is the release of life from the limitations of matter.
Joy	The joy of the Lord is the transfiguration of life.
Creation	The creation of life is the birth of the Lord.
Truth	The truth of light is the life of the Self-Illumined Light of God.

Radiance	The radiant Self-Illumined Light of God invites the consciousness of matter to life.
Illumination	The illumined light of forever welcomes you to the source of life.
Beyond	The transcendental material of God is the substance of life.
Unity	The salvation of life is the unity of the Self-Illumined Light of God.

Illumination

Love	The solar lights of God invoke the grand awakening in the body of God.
Peace	The exalted light of God is the liberating force of life.
Light	The awakened souls of the Lord are the ambassadors of the Self-Illumined Light of God.
Joy	The joyous celebration of the children of God form the dance of light.
Creation	The creative spark of the eternal expansion of God is the force of life.
Truth	The truth of God is the inherent life in the Self-Illumined Light Body of God.
Radiance	The radiant Son of God is the sole life in the universe of God.
Illumination	The one relationship in God is the reality of the Self-Illumined Light of God.

Beyond	The transcendental material of God is the Self-Illumined Light Body of God.
Unity	The unity of God is the life of the Self-Illumined Light of God.

Beyond

Love	The transcendental light of God exists at the center of consciousness.
Peace	A single focus of divine intention opened the door of splendor.
Light	The effulgent light of God emanated out of the ecstasy of grace.
Joy	The rapture of intense joy merged consciousness into the creation of angels.
Creation	The Kingdom of God descended into the manifestation of the universe.
Truth	The eternal reverberations of divine consciousness unfolded the reality of the Self-Illumined Light of God.
Radiance	The radiant heart of the Self-Illumined Light of God guides the destiny of the children of God.
Illumination	The awakened body of God reveals the truth of life in the eternity of ascension.
Beyond	The ascended light in the Self-Illumined Light Body of God is the new material of life.
Unity	God material is the body of unity in the dimension of form.

Unity

Love	A single focus of light gathered into the space of God.
Peace	In a moment of solitude the presence of God was revealed.
Light	A single ray of light connected the form of God.
Joy	The angels manifested out of the form of God.
Creation	In an instant, creation emerged out of the light of God.
Truth	The truth of eternity expressed the power of light.
Radiance	The radiant light of God emerged from the center of existence.
Illumination	The illumined presence of eternity released unions of light.
Beyond	The transcendence of God emerged from the silence.
Unity	The unity of God revealed the totality.

Splendor

Love	The splendor of light released light into the sea of everlasting joy.
Peace	The joy of splendor filled light with the peace of God.

Light	The peace of God filled the universe with eternal light.
Joy	From the light of God, joy descended into the peace of eternal light.
Creation	Creation emerged from the sacred union of light and love.
Truth	The truth of infinity released immortality into the ocean of life.
Radiance	Radiant light filled space with the rapture of eternal life.
Illumination	The illumined light of God entered life on wings of golden star crystals.
Beyond	The transcendent crystals of light reveal the lattice of everlasting being.
Unity	The everlasting presence of God reveals the union of light.

Purity

Love	I am light.
Peace	God is light.
Light	The universe is light.
Joy	I am joy.
Creation	God created light.

Truth	The light of God is joy.
Radiance	Joy radiates light.
Illumination	Joy is the knower of light.
Beyond	Light is the knower of joy.
Unity	Joy is light.

The Birth of God
The Emergence of Light

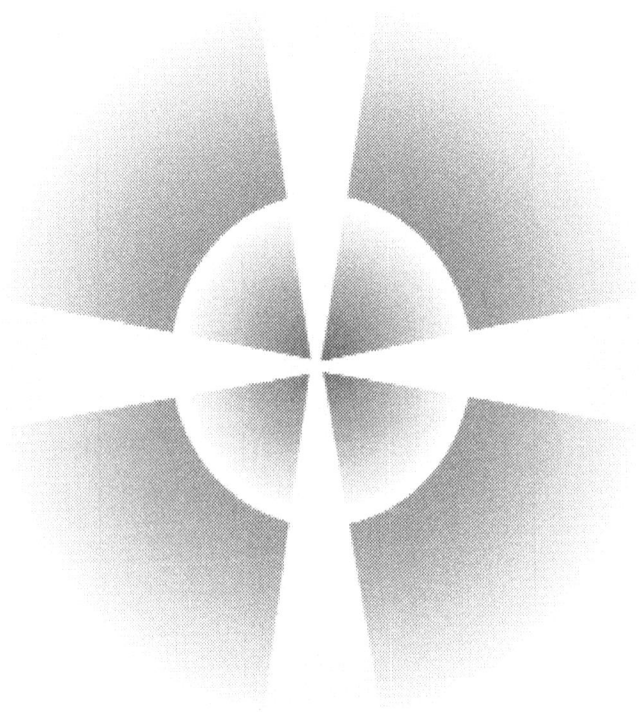

Love

Love	A child of God is born in a manger of light.
Peace	The light has come to take away the darkness.
Light	The birth of God is the transformation from darkness to light.
Joy	The resurrection of light is the celebration of the heavenly hosts of God.
Creation	The manger of matter fulfills the divine plan of God.
Truth	The transformation of light into matter is the truth of God.
Radiance	The radiation of light from material reality is the life of God.
Illumination	The living material of divine intelligence becomes the body of God.
Beyond	The transcendence of God becomes the living substance of divine matter.
Unity	The union of light and matter form the birth of God.

Peace

Love	The waiting events of the Self-Illumined Light of God are gathered together into an expanding body of light.

Peace	The events of the Self-Illumined Light of God form the connecting links in the body of light.
Light	The connecting links of the Self-Illumined Light of God form a tapestry of the relationships of light.
Joy	A tapestry of golden crystals light the universe with infinite joy.
Creation	Creation emerged from endless rays of golden light.
Truth	Starlit skies formed a canopy of eternal light.
Radiance	The light of God radiated from the joy of eternal love.
Illumination	Eternal love illumined the life of the Son of God.
Beyond	The transcendence of God emerged from the peace of eternity.
Unity	The union of light and love entered the life of God.

Light

Love	Light releases love into space.
Peace	Space releases peace into light.
Light	God releases light into space.
Joy	Joy releases love into life.
Creation	Life releases joy into light.
Truth	Truth releases creation into love.

Radiance	Radiance releases love into light.
Illumination	Illumination releases light into eternity.
Beyond	Transcendence releases silence into infinity.
Unity	Unity releases life into God.

Joy

Love	Joy emerged out of the crown of God.
Peace	The throne of God filled space with the splendor of light.
Light	The fountain of light poured love into the Kingdom of God.
Joy	Peace awoke inviting the Son of God.
Creation	On wings of light the Son of Peace entered the universe of God.
Truth	The universe revealed the birth of God.
Radiance	The joy of light created the tapestry of God.
Illumination	The power of God transformed life into light.
Beyond	Light revealed the eternity of God.
Unity	Illumined by light, the transcendence of God revealed the unification of consciousness.

Creation

Love	The sacred event of light lifted life into the ascension of God.
Peace	The peace of God created light from the union of love and peace.
Light	The creation of light merged joy into creation.
Joy	The birth of joy filled life with the presence of God.
Creation	Creation emerged from the sun of everlasting joy.
Truth	The joy of light entered the city of God.
Radiance	From the radiant heart of eternity, the Son of God is born.
Illumination	The birth of God is the light of eternity in the space of infinite joy.
Beyond	Joy emerges from the transcendent light of God.
Unity	Unity is born from the transcendence of light.

Truth

Love	Created from the sun of everlasting truth, the rising child of God ascends to the throne of salvation.
Peace	The Throne of Light gives power and strength to the children of the sacred word.

Light	The sacred word of God fills eternity with pulsations of living light.
Joy	Pulsating forms of God deliver the sacred sounds of eternity to the children of light.
Creation	The sacred sounds of eternity invoke the manifestation of light.
Truth	Manifested out of the mouth of God, the vibration of light gave birth to the Son of God.
Radiance	The radiant child of eternity opened the light of God, revealing the path to immortality.
Illumination	Awakened by the illumined light of God, the child of eternity ascends to the Throne of Salvation.
Beyond	The salvation of light lifts the children of God into the unification of light.
Unity	The union of eternal light reveals the totality of God.

Radiance

Love	From the radiant sun of eternal light, the power of God lifts consciousness into the ascension of light.
Peace	The ascending lights of God form the body of eternal light, responsible for the creation of God.
Light	The movement of light embraced the power of God, filling the spaces of consciousness with the glorification of light.
Joy	The glorification of light guides the unification of

consciousness, manifesting the totality of God.

Creation	Created by the presence of living light, the children of God awaken the consciousness of light.
Truth	Manifested by the power of God, the children of eternity form the continuous stream of awakening splendor.
Radiance	The radiant forms of eternity create the living material of light.
Illumination	The illumined material of light forms the conscious realities of God.
Beyond	The transcendent material of light is the body of God.
Unity	The material of unity is the divine substance of immortality.

Illumination

Love	The illumined lights of eternity open the incarnation of light to the children of God.
Peace	The incarnating lights of eternity fill the spaces of God with the presence of eternal love.
Light	Resurrected in the continuum of space, the Son of God incarnates into material reality.
Joy	The rising child of eternity is the living presence of God.
Creation	Formed from the flame of immortality, God reveals

the incarnation of light.

Truth   Purged in the flame of immortality, God reveals the truth of manifestation.

Radiance   Emancipated by the flame of immortality, God opens the salvation of light.

Illumination   Illumined by the flame of immortality, God awakens the children of light.

Beyond   Freed by the flame of immortality, God activates the sounds of immortality.

Unity   Opened by the flame of immortality, God creates The New Jerusalem of Light.

Beyond

Love   The emergence of light fills space with the transcendence of God.

Peace   The anointed of God transcend the limitation of space.

Light   The resurrection of light is the formation of transcendent realities of God.

Joy   The transcendent realities of light are created from the joy of God.

Creation   The sanctity of light reverberates in the spaces of God.

Truth   The truth of God is the power of light.

Radiance	The radiant heart of God expands into the eternity of space.
Illumination	The illumined seraphim reveal the order of God.
Beyond	The transcendence of God is the order of light.
Unity	The order of light is the unification of God.

Unity

Love	The union of light is born in the dimension of love.
Peace	The peace of God is revealed in the dimension of love.
Light	The light of God is resurrected in the dimension of love.
Joy	The joy of God is celebrated in the dimension of love.
Creation	The creation of God is manifested in the dimension of love.
Truth	The truth of God is lived in the dimension of love.
Radiance	The radiance of God is magnified in the dimension of love.
Illumination	The illumination of God is known in the dimension of love.
Beyond	The transcendence of God is visible in the dimension of love.
Unity	The unity of God is fulfilled in the dimension of love.

Splendor

Love
The light eternal raises the children of God into the ascending stream of God.

Peace
The ascending stream of light manifests the continuum of revelations that generate the body of God.

Light
The revelation of God forms the universe of light responsible for administrating the sacred events of God.

Joy
The joy of light is the continuous celebration of the sacred events of God.

Creation
Creation forms the sequential unfolding realities of the revelations of God.

Truth
The realities of light represent the truth found in the reverberations of consciousness.

Radiance
Consciousness radiates from the center of light causing patterns of light to reveal the splendor of existence.

Illumination
Consciousness awakens in the infinity of space manifesting continuous streams of light.

Beyond
The transcendent streams of light form the expanding universe of God.

Unity
The universe of God lives at the center of light.

Purity

Love	The purity of God exists at the center of light.
Peace	The purity of God lives in the forms of light.
Light	The purity of God reveals the universe of light.
Joy	The purity of God celebrates the joy of light.
Creation	The purity of God manifests the structures of light.
Truth	The purity of God forms the power of light.
Radiance	The purity of God radiates the eternity of light.
Illumination	The purity of God illuminates the body of light.
Beyond	The purity of God expands the transcendence of light.
Unity	The purity of God unifies the children of light.

The Tapestry of God
The Connectivity of Light

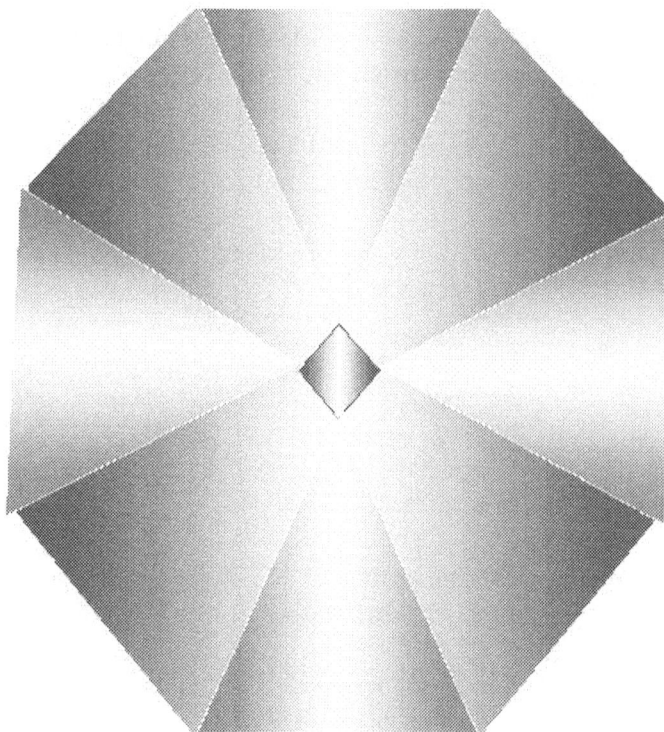

Love

Love	The sounds of the Self-Illumined Light of God form the tapestry of God.
Peace	The vibrations of the Self-Illumined Light of God form the tapestry of God.
Light	The light of the Self-Illumined Light of God forms the tapestry of God.
Joy	The joy of the Self-Illumined Light of God forms the tapestry of God.
Creation	The hands of the Self-Illumined Light of God form the tapestry of God.
Truth	The truth of the Self-Illumined Light of God forms the tapestry of God.
Radiance	The radiance of the Self-Illumined Light of God forms the tapestry of God.
Illumination	The illumination of the Self-Illumined Light of God forms the tapestry of God.
Beyond	The splendor of the Self-Illumined Light of God forms the tapestry of God.
Unity	The purity of the Self-Illumined Light of God forms the tapestry of God.

Peace

Love	The soft breezes of love form the tapestry of God.
Peace	The soft breezes of peace form the tapestry of God.
Light	The soft breezes of light form the tapestry of God.
Joy	The soft breezes of joy form the tapestry of God.
Creation	The soft breezes of touch form the tapestry of God.
Truth	The soft breezes of truth form the tapestry of God.
Radiance	The soft breezes of eternity form the tapestry of God.
Illumination	The soft breezes of illumination form the tapestry of God.
Beyond	The soft breezes of transcendence form the tapestry of God.
Unity	The soft breezes of purity form the tapestry of God.

Light

Love	The sounds of God weave the fabric of eternity into the form of light.
Peace	The ancients of light form the material of eternal life.
Light	In the sacred time of light, the deliverer awakens the souls of eternal life.

Joy	In the sacred hour, the rapture of light transforms life into the living material of light.
Creation	We are the creative forces of transformation.
Truth	The heart of God is the nutrient of light.
Radiance	The body of God is the salvation of life.
Illumination	The resurrection of God is the liberation of the soul.
Beyond	The transcendence of God is the majesty of life.
Unity	The unity of God is the covenant of light.

———

Joy

Love	The love of God fills the heart with the joy of light.
Peace	The joy of light is the fabric of life.
Light	The joy of God is the consciousness of light.
Joy	The light of God is the foundation of life.
Creation	The foundation of God is the structure of light.
Truth	The structure of light reveals the dynamics of God.
Radiance	The dynamics of God reveals the nature of existence.
Illumination	The nature of existence finds fulfillment in the light of God.
Beyond	The light of God reveals the transcendental nature of life.
Unity	The nature of life is the unity of God.

Creation

Love	I created the world from the one reality.
Peace	I gave birth to the one life.
Light	I resurrected the one light.
Joy	I revealed the one joy.
Creation	I fulfill the one life.
Truth	I speak the one truth.
Radiance	I radiate the one light.
Illumination	I illuminate the one thought.
Beyond	I open the one door.
Unity	I am the one God.

Truth

Love	I am the breath of truth living in the space of God.
Peace	I am the breath of peace living in the space of God.
Light	I am the breath of light living in the space of God.
Joy	I am the breath of joy living in the space of God.
Creation	I am the breath of creation living in the space of God.

Truth	I am the breath of God living in the space of light.
Radiance	I am the breath of radiance living in the space of God.
Illumination	I am the breath of illumination living in the space of God.
Beyond	I am the breath of transcendence living in the space of God.
Unity	I am the breath of unity living in the space of God.

Radiance

Love	The radiant form of God expands across the fabric of time.
Peace	The sequences of time weave the garment of life.
Light	Light gathers the sequences of time into units of eternity.
Joy	The units of eternity open space to the structures of light.
Creation	The structures of light awaken the fabrics of time to the eternity of God.
Truth	The fabrics of time remember the sequential order of the structures of light.
Radiance	The memory of God is carried across the fabrics of time.
Illumination	The illumination of light awakens the fabrics of

THE BOOK OF THE HOLY LIGHT

	time to the eternity of light.
Beyond	The memories of light are released into the eternity of space.
Unity	The memory of God is unified in the reality of God.

Illumination

Love	The luminaries of God are the emissaries of light.
Peace	They carry the throne of peace to the children of God.
Light	They deliver the song of God to the children of light.
Joy	They rise in a chorus of light emanations from the heart of God.
Creation	They are the creators of form in the body of God.
Truth	Their love forms the temple of God.
Radiance	Their radiance fills the temple of God with the light of eternity.
Illumination	They illuminate the spaces of God with the thoughts of eternal life.
Beyond	They envision the opened door of salvation in the eternity of God.
Unity	They reveal the presence of the redeemer of light.

Beyond

Love	Beyond the threads of time the living presence of God forms the unions of eternal life.
Peace	In the spaces of His love the song of eternal life finds peace in the heart of God.
Light	Whoever hears the song of life is filled with the light of God.
Joy	Whoever sings the songs of God will find joy in the life of God.
Creation	Whoever walks with the Son of God will find a home in the body of God.
Truth	I live in the fabric of time and create in the spaces of God.
Radiance	I am the living presence of God, the salvation of eternal life.
Illumination	Whoever believes in me will inherit the life of God.
Beyond	I am the word of God, the message of love
Unity	I am the testament of His life.

Unity

Love	The unity of our Lord is the thread that binds the children of light to the sacred event of the living God.

Peace	The sacred event of our Lord is the living material of light.
Light	The living material of light is the body of God.
Joy	The resurrection of our Lord is the manifestation of the life of God.
Creation	The life of God is the presence of the Son of God.
Truth	The life of our Lord is revealed in the material of light.
Radiance	The material of light is the life of the Son of God.
Illumination	The Son of God is the light of eternal life.
Beyond	Eternal life is the living material of light.
Unity	I am the body of eternal life.

Splendor

Love	The life of our Lord is given for the pain of our heart.
Peace	The life of our lord has risen for the resurrection of our heart.
Light	The love of our Lord is received for the liberation of our heart.
Joy	The joy of our Lord is celebrated in the peace of our heart.
Creation	The existence of our Lord is revealed in the depth of our heart.

Truth	The truth of our Lord is shared in the silence of our heart.
Radiance	The faith of our Lord is revealed with the touch of His heart.
Illumination	The light of our Lord is seen at the center of our heart.
Beyond	The transcendence of our Lord is felt through the knowing in our heart.
Unity	The unity of our Lord is embraced with the love of our heart.

Purity

Love	The pure form of God is the realty of light.
Peace	The realty of light translates the pure form of God into the material of light.
Light	The material of light translates the reality of God into the form of God.
Joy	The form of God is transformed into the sounds of eternal life.
Creation	The sounds of eternal life are the ascending realities of light.
Truth	The ascending realities of light contain the messages of eternal life.
Radiance	The messages of eternal life radiate the love of God.

Illumination	The love of God awakens the soul to the reality of eternal life.
Beyond	The reality of eternal life is the spirit of God in the temple of the soul.
Unity	The temple of the soul is the sacred event of eternity transfigured in the ascension of light.

The Power of God
The Redemption of Light

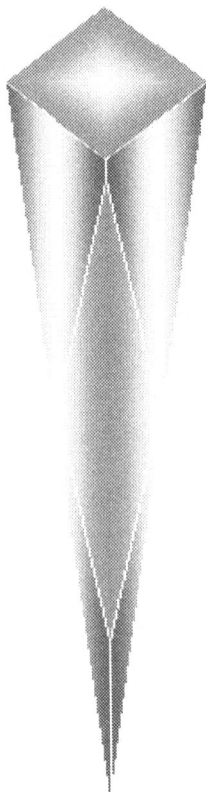

Love

Love	The power of God lives at the center of life.
Peace	The power of light creates from the center of life.
Light	The power of love manifests light from the center of life.
Joy	The power of love manifests joy from the center of life.
Creation	The power of love manifests form from the center of life.
Truth	The power of love manifests truth from the center of life.
Radiance	The power of love manifests radiance from the center of life.
Illumination	The power of love manifests illumination from the center of life.
Beyond	The power of love manifests transcendence from the center of life.
Unity	The power of love manifests unity from the center of life.

Peace

Love	The creation of life is the power of God.

Peace	The presence of peace is the power of God.
Light	The manifestation of light is the power of God.
Joy	The lifting of hearts is the power of God.
Creation	The manifestation of form is the power of God.
Truth	The revelation of truth is the power of God.
Radiance	The radiance of truth is the power of God.
Illumination	The illumination of truth is the power of God.
Beyond	The transcendence of truth is the power of God.
Unity	The unity of truth is the power of God.

Light

Love	The power of God comes from the love of God.
Peace	The power of God comes from the peace of God.
Light	The power of God comes from the light of God.
Joy	The power of God comes from the joy of God.
Creation	The power of God comes from the touch of God.
Truth	The power of God comes from the truth of God.
Radiance	The power of God comes from the radiance of God.
Illumination	The power of God comes from the illumination of God.

THE BOOK OF THE HOLY LIGHT

Beyond	The power of God comes from the transcendence of God.
Unity	The power of God comes from the unity of God.

Joy

Love	Joy is the power of God.
Peace	Peace is the power of God.
Light	Light is the power of God.
Joy	Rapture is the power of God.
Creation	Creation is the power of God.
Truth	Truth is the power of God.
Radiance	Radiance is the power of God.
Illumination	Illumination is the power of God.
Beyond	Knowledge is the power of God.
Unity	Unity is the power of God.

Creation

Love	The love of the Father is the sacrament of eternal life.
Peace	His eternal presence lifts the awakening heart revealing the truth of the ascended realities of God.
Light	The ascended realities of light shape the landscape of

eternal life.

Joy	Lifted by the grace of God, the children of light enter the landscape of eternal life.
Creation	Guided by the Son of God, the children of light are revealed in the landscape of eternal life.
Truth	Resurrected by the power of God, the children of light inherit the landscape of eternal life.
Radiance	The inherited landscape of eternal life fills space with invisible laws of light.
Illumination	The laws of light illuminate the landscape of eternal life.
Beyond	The transcendence of God is the material of the land scape of eternal life.
Unity	The unity of God is the reality of the landscape of eternal life.

Truth

Love	I deliver the light of God to the children of eternal life.
Peace	I deliver the peace of God to the children of eternal life.
Light	I deliver the power of God to the children of eternal life.
Joy	I deliver the joy of God to the children of eternal life.

Creation	I deliver the touch of God to the children of eternal life.
Truth	I deliver the truth of God to the children of eternal life.
Radiance	I deliver the radiance of God to the children of eternal life.
Illumination	I deliver the illumination of God to the children of eternal life.
Beyond	I deliver the transcendence of God to the children of eternal life.
Unity	I deliver the unity of God to the children of eternal life.

Radiance

Love	The radiant universe of God transforms life into living light.
Peace	The radiant universe of God transforms peace into the material of light.
Light	The radiant universe of God transforms light into material reality.
Joy	The radiant universe of God transforms joy into material form.
Creation	The radiant universe of God transforms creation into the material of light.
Truth	The radiant universe of God transforms truth into

the temple of God.

Radiance   The radiant universe of God is transformed by grace into the cities of eternal life.

Illumination   The radiant universe of God is transformed by illumination into the cities of eternal life.

Beyond   The radiant universe of God is transformed by silence into the cities of eternal life.

Unity   The radiant universe of God is transformed by unity into the cities of eternal life.

Illumination

Love   Light streams cleanse the thoughts of eternity, awakening the spirit of God in the soul of eternal life.

Peace   Awakened in the spirit of God, the soul of eternal life ascends to the throne of light.

Light   Transformed in the awakening light of God, the offspring of light becomes the inheritor of His grace.

Joy   The witness to eternal life opens his heart to the grace of God.

Creation   The touch of grace transforms the witness of light into the life of God.

Truth   The truth of His grace reveals the opening to eternal life.

Radiance   The radiance of His grace illuminates the opening to eternal life.

Illumination	The illumination of His grace forms the opening to eternal life.
Beyond	The transcendence of His grace creates the opening to eternal life.
Unity	The unity of His grace is the opening to eternal life.

Beyond

Love	Transcendent joy radiated from the heart of God, forming the pathways of light.
Peace	The living God entered the pathways of divine incarnation, forming the living streams of material light.
Light	The streams of material light flow outward, forming living realities of divine incarnations.
Joy	The formations of light realities open the door of eternal life.
Creation	The invitation of light welcomes the spirit of God in the form of the eternal Son.
Truth	Blessed are the children who walk in the direction of God.
Radiance	Blessed are the children who enter the Kingdom of God.
Illumination	Blessed are the children who hear the name of the Lord.
Beyond	Blessed are the children who receive the inheritance of the Lord.

Unity	Blessed are the children who ascend to the throne of God.

Unity

Love	The union of the eternal flame of consciousness ignites the transformation into the order of the Son of God.
Peace	The order of light is the destiny of the evolution of life from inception to liberation.
Light	The order of light calls you home to eternal life.
Joy	The order of light frees your spirit to the eternal Son.
Creation	The order of light guides the loving heart to the ocean of the eternal song.
Truth	The order of light is the song of eternal life.
Radiance	The order of light is the radiant Son of God.
Illumination	The order of light illuminates the spaces of God opening the doorway to eternal life.
Beyond	The order of light is the universal key to eternal life.
Unity	The order of light is the ascending stream of eternal life.

Splendor

Love   The splendor of light is the call of eternity to the children of God.

Peace   Whispered on the breath of God, the sounds of eternal life take form in the body of God.

Light   The heart of light feels the presence of eternal life.

Joy   The heart of light feels the joy of eternal life.

Creation   The heart of light feels the touch of eternal life.

Truth   The heart of light feels the truth of eternal life.

Radiance   The heart of light feels the radiance of eternal life.

Illumination   The heart of light feels the illumination of eternal life.

Beyond   The heart of light feels the transcendence of eternal life.

Unity   The heart of light feels the unity of eternal life.

Purity

Love   The opened eye of God visualized the forms of God.

Peace   The opened eye of God visualized the peace of God.

Light   The opened eye of God visualized the light of God.

Joy	The opened eye of God visualized the joy of God.
Creation	The opened eye of God visualized the creation of God.
Truth	The opened eye of God visualized the truth of God.
Radiance	The opened eye of God visualized the radiance of God.
Illumination	The opened eye of God visualized the illumination of God.
Beyond	The opened eye of God visualized the transcendence of God.
Unity	The opened eye of God visualized the unity of God.